D1244880

Healing with
Astrology

by Marcia Starck

THE CROSSING PRESS
FREEDOM, CALIFORNIA

For information on bulk purchases or group discounts for this and other Crossing Press titles, please contact our Special Sales Manager at 800–777–1048 x214. Visit our Web site on the Internet at: www.crossingpress.com

Healing and medicine are two very different disciplines, and the law requires the following disclaimer. The information in this book is not medicine but healing, and it does not constitute medical advice. In case of serious illness consult the practitioner of your choice.

ISBN 0–89594–862–1

Author Services

**Your may contact Marcia Starck,
Medical Astrologer at:**

Earth Medicine Ways
P. O. Box 5435
Santa Fe, NM 87502
(505) 473-1464

This book is dedicated to three great Earth Mothers:
my grandmother Rose Kaplan and my dear friend
Frida Waterhouse, both of whom have passed on to another plane,
and my mother Helen Cantor.

Special thanks to Judith Pynn, my editor at The Crossing Press, for helping to birth *Healing with Astrology*. I also want to thank Elaine Goldman Gill, my publisher, for her continued support. In addition, I thank the art department at The Crossing Press for their inspiration in designing this book.

For help with the information contained in this book, I am grateful to Richard and Patricia Katz of the Flower Essence Society of Nevada City, CA; Kathi Keville, a wonderful herbalist from Nevada City, CA; Lawrence "White Elk" Loving for taking me deeper into the mysteries of the crystal kingdom; and the beautiful Sierra Nevadas for sustaining my vision during much of the original writing of this book.

Contents

Foreword

It is significant that *Healing with Astrology* be published as we prepare for the next millennium. Since the 1960s we have witnessed many old forms of healing being revived as the natural healing movement gained momentum. We have also witnessed increased awareness concerning the healing of the Earth and the beginnings of the eco-feminism movement.

Through understanding the Gaia hypothesis, which postulates that the Earth herself is a living, breathing organism who feels the decimation, pillage, and rape to her being, we have connected her experiences to our own bodies. This connection has made us increasingly aware of what is "natural" (made from natural organic elements) and what is "synthetic." From vitamins and minerals to household cleaning products, we have substituted natural ingredients for chemical ones.

In the 1980s we had several significant planetary alignments. First, there was the Harmonic Convergence of August 15–16, 1987, with seven planets in fire signs indicating the purifying and destructive energies. The Harmonic Convergence was based on the cycles of the ancient Mayan calendar, which synchronized with many of the Hopi prophecies. In 1988 we had the Saturn-Uranus conjunction in the last degree of Sagittarius, almost in Capricorn. That inaugurated the beginning of strong Earth changes and was followed by a Saturn-Neptune conjunction in Capricorn in 1989. The structure of Saturn was dissolved by Neptune. With Neptune in Capricorn (where it is as of this writing), we became missionaries to spiritualize the Earth and bring her back into a state of balance and equilibrium.

In 1989 my book *Earth Mother Astrology* was published. Much of the original book is included in *Healing with Astrology*. *Earth Mother Astrology* was a book that heralded the 1990s bringing together the awareness of both the sky (the study of Astrology) and the Earth (the study of herbs, flowers, crystals). Earth Mother Astrology is about the Sacred Marriage, the balance that we strive for as we work on our female/male polarity and harmonize the energies within us. This sacred marriage exists on three levels: it exists within each of us as we work to balance our own female and male; it exists in society as women and men work together in creating harmony and peace; and it exists on the cosmic level in the balance between Earth Mother and Sky Father. When all three of these are in harmony, we are in tune with natural law.

Utilizing Earth Mother Astrology, which is similar to alchemical principles, we study the stars to determine which influences we are under and what might help to balance our bodies as we are hit by transits of the outer planets and progressions. Each of us is a unique being with our own energy field. Each of us was born on a certain day in a specific city and country. The configurations in the heavens on that day at that time and place are symbols of the energies we have chosen to work with in this lifetime and account for our personality traits, strengths and weaknesses, and physical sensitivities.

Just as each human being is governed by these planetary configurations, so too is the plant kingdom. Plants bloom in certain seasons and wither and die at other times. Gathering of special herbs is performed at certain times of the year and specific times of the day. A plant is influenced by planetary influences just as we are; thus, certain plants make good medicines for various individuals. This is also true of crystals and gems that grow beneath the Earth's surface. They too are influenced by planetary vibrations and therefore harmonize with certain temperaments.

The foods we eat are different colors, contain various nutritional substances, and have certain aromas. We may need particular nutrients when we come under the influence of specific planetary cycles; under Uranus, for example, we need more B-complex vitamins and the minerals magnesium and manganese to balance our nervous system.

Through the vibrations of sound and color we can transform our emotional states and attune ourselves to flow in harmony with the Earth's changes. Uranus is now in Aquarius, and we are working with more and more subtle forms of healing. Sound, which is perhaps our oldest form of healing, has become one of the strongest healing modalities now in use. The ancient art of drumming has returned, with many kinds of drums used for different rhythms. The drum is, in fact, the heart beat or the beat of the Earth Mother. Drumming really gained momentum with the Uranus-Neptune conjunction in Capricorn in 1993. Toning, chanting, the use of different sounds to work with various chakras, have all been increasing. Sounds associated with various planets are now being used to work with various pathologies in the body and psyche. Utilizing color and light in working with imbalances in the body and psyche have also been known since the beginning of time. Art therapy has become a major tool in working to bring back harmony into the physical and mental realms.

With the Jupiter-Uranus conjunction in Aquarius in February 1997, the natural approaches to healing that were developed in the 1960s are being spread to the rest of the world. Knowledge of Astrology is also spreading as more and more individuals become aware of cosmic cycles and gain a deeper understanding of their role within the larger galaxy. To work deeper with these cycles—monthly, seasonal, and yearly—we need group ceremonies and rituals. Rituals open us to receive the energies of Earth Mother and Sky Father and to commune with each other in a more transpersonal way. At each New Moon and Full Moon, each equinox and solstice, we have an opportunity to bring healing to ourselves as well as the Earth, as we rebalance and realign the energies.

Introduction

How to Use This Book

This book is designed to be used with an accurately calculated horoscope if you have one, but may also be used to attune to the energies at various times of the year. For example, during the time of Virgo (August 21–September 20) there may be certain herbs that are appropriate, or flower essences, as we collectively attune to the cosmic energy of Virgo. (Clearing our digestive tracts and purifying our emotions would be examples of Virgo.)

In order to obtain an accurate horoscope, you can contact any professional astrologer or reputable astrological computing service.

One needs to know three factors in order to have a natal chart cast—date of birth, time of birth, and place of birth. For those who don't know their specific time, there are departments in the state capitols (if one is born in the United States) where one can write and obtain this information. (The Department of Health, Education and Welfare publishes a pamphlet called "Where to Write for Birth and Death Records." To obtain this pamphlet, send $5.00 to Superintendent of Documents, U.S. Government Printing Office, Washington, D.C. 20402 and ask for DHEW Pub. No. 76-1142.)

Some professional astrologers are also able to rectify the time of birth by obtaining a series of important events in one's life and specific dates that correspond. Once the natal horoscope is calculated, yearly progressions and transits can be done to understand the cycles through which an individual is currently going.

If you only know your Sun sign, you can look up information about that sign and its ruling planet in the chapter on signs. Once you know the planet that rules your Sun sign, you can then utilize the other chapters in this book by looking up the vitamins and minerals ruled by that planet and the herbs, crystals and gems, aromas, colors, and musical notes associated with it. Flower essences are listed under the signs and not the planets. However, this is a general way to utilize the information and may not mean that you need those particular things.

The more accurate way to do this is to have the complete horoscope calculated and then follow the steps in the rest of this chapter. In working with a holistic framework, we know that each of us is very individual and has needs and imbalances that are different from others. The horoscope provides us with a "cosmic photograph" of what those needs are. In addition, it is helpful to utilize any tools such as dowsing with a pendulum or muscle testing to confirm that the particular herb or flower essence is appropriate for us at any given time. Utilizing iridology, pulse diagnosis, and other holistic diagnostic modalities along with the horoscope provide even more information.

How Holistic Astrology Applies to Your Horoscope

The case histories in the last chapter of this book illustrate how the information contained in the other chapters can be utilized with your personal horoscope. The following paragraphs explain how you can use this information once you've had an accurate horoscope calculated.

By analyzing the natal horoscope in relation to correspondences with the elements described in this book, we can determine how to harmonize our physical vehicles so that we may walk in balance on the Earth Mother. According to the laws of metaphysics, many of the imbalances in the physical body are a result of inharmonious conditions existing in the higher vehicles—the emotional, mental, and causal bodies. Science explains imbalances of the physical vehicle through hereditary factors and genetic history. The complete picture probably encompasses both of these points of view. Many books on the mind/body connection describe this phenomenon. For example, Dr. Hans Selye in *The Stress of Life* (McGraw-Hill, 1976) showed all the physiological changes the body undergoes when subjected to various types of stress. In their work with cancer, Carl and Stephanie Simonton also showed the emotional factors leading to cellular changes within the RNA/DNA code.

How then do we determine these physiological imbalances through a study of the natal horoscope? The important point to remember is that the horoscope only indicates *potential* imbalances; the stresses we are under at the time, how much we exercise, the type of food we eat, and the way we take care of our body determine our state of health and balance.

In studying the horoscope, we first make an **element analysis** determining if there is an excess or lack of any elements. Excess air, for example, indicates that the nervous system needs attention. We would then see which planets and signs are related to air and the nervous system. Here we find particularly

Mercury and Uranus, as well as the signs Gemini, Libra, and Aquarius and houses three, seven, and eleven. Looking up Mercury and Uranus in the various chapters, we find that they are associated with certain minerals like magnesium and manganese, the B complex vitamins, the nervine herbs (herbs like chamomile, catnip, and spearmint that are used to balance the nervous system), and such crystals and gems as lapis lazuli and blue tourmaline. Another example might be a lack of fire, indicating few planets in the signs Aries, Leo, Sagittarius, the planets Mars, the Sun, and Jupiter in weak positions in the horoscope, and a lack of planets in the first, fifth, and ninth houses. Studying the various chapters, we find that Mars is associated with iron, the Sun with vitamin D, and Jupiter with silica. We also find that certain herbs mentioned under these planets like cayenne and ginger build up fire within the body as do gemstones like bloodstone, carnelian and ruby.

After examining the elements, one looks at the rest of the horoscope. Is there a **conglomeration of planets** in one sign or one house? If so, this may indicate a weakness physiologically as well as psychologically. For example, with three or four planets in Libra, one may need to work on relationships; one may also tend to have weak kidneys. There are some herbs listed under Venus that are helpful to the kidneys, and the bioflavonoids, which contain rutin, are also beneficial. Three or four planets in the seventh house, which has a similar vibration to Libra, may have an analogous effect but not quite as strong.

Next the **Sun, Moon, and Ascendant** and how they are aspected need to be studied to determine the basic vitality. Aspects are the mathematical distances between planets. Hard aspects include the opposition (180 degrees), the square (90 degrees), and the semisquare (45 degrees), as well as combinations of these such as the sesquiquadrate (135 degrees). These aspects, including the conjunction (when two planets occupy the same degree), and the quincunx or inconjunct (150 degrees), a first/sixth house aspect, should be primarily considered. The soft aspects such as trines (120 degrees), sextiles (60 degrees), and semi-sextiles (30 degrees) do not cause imbalances themselves but may facilitate any complexes that exist, or may simply provide some relief to the hard aspects. A person with a Capricorn Moon, for example, may tend to lack calcium, especially if there are many hard aspects to Saturn, the ruler of Capricorn. A Scorpio Sun individual with hard aspects to Pluto, ruler of Scorpio, may tend to need more vitamin E or selenium or some of the herbs or flower remedies under Scorpio.

In regard to health and personal habits, any planets in the **sixth house** should be considered, as well as the ruler of the sixth. Where is it placed and how is it aspected? The sign Sagittarius on the cusp with its ruler Jupiter squared by Saturn might mean possible problems with the liver and pancreas and lowered bile production. (Bile is produced by the liver, ruled by Jupiter, and stored in the gallbladder, ruled by Saturn.) Jupiter herbs, such as dandelion root and chicory may be important, as well as stones like turquoise or chrysocolla.

Lastly, the **T-squares** in the horoscope (two planets opposite each other squaring a third) are important in indicating areas of tension and imbalance. Venus opposite Saturn square Mars may show a person who holds back energy and the expression of emotions. Venus rules Taurus, which governs the thyroid, and this might suggest the lack of iodine. The individual also may need some flower remedies associated with Taurus or Libra, the other sign ruled by Venus, such as iris or penstemon, and crystals like rose quartz or pink tourmaline.

After a study of the natal horoscope has been completed, it is important to look at current **progressions and transits** to determine what cycles one is in and how the energy is being affected. Under Uranus transits, there might be a lot of changes that affect the nervous system; utilizing minerals as magnesium and manganese and colors in the blue spectrum might be helpful. Neptune transits would make the individual more open psychically and affect the immune system with possible allergies or low blood sugar. Utilizing extra potassium, flower remedies such as clematis and lotus, or the crystals amethyst, fluorite, or sugilite would be beneficial.

Since the horoscope indicates potential imbalances, it is helpful to have a system of confirmation. There are many good systems linked with alternative healing modalities. Personally, the one I find that works well in conjunction with the horoscope is radiesthesia, the science of detecting vibrations through the use of a pendulum or dowsing rod. In using radiesthesia, one can determine which chakras (centers of energy on the higher bodies) are out of balance, which physical organs need work, and what vitamin or mineral deficiencies exist. One can also double-check any herbs, flower remedies, colors, or gems and crystals that have been suggested from the natal chart. Utilizing a pendulum, this can be done with either a list of the herbs or flower remedies or crystals, or by holding the pendulum over the suggested herbs, vitamins, vials of flower essences, or crystals.

Another good confirmation tool includes muscle testing or applied kinesiology, which works by holding the herb or vitamin bottle or crystal and checking the strength of the muscles before and after, to see whether the substance strengthens or depletes the body. Other diagnostic systems include iridology, the study of the iris of the eye, and pulse taking in Asian medicine.

TABLE OF ASSOCIATIONS

Planet	Vitamins & Minerals	Foods	Herbs
☉	D, gold	sunshine, fish liver oils	hawthorn, lily of the valley, lavender
☽	silver	dairy products, tofu	mugwort, hops
☿	B complex	whole grains	nervine herbs, catnip, scullcap
♀	iodine, copper	sea vegetables, fish	dandelion leaf, uva ursi, alfalfa, licorice, anise
♂	iron	dulse, liver, beets, blackstrap molasses, wheatgrass juice	nettles, yellow dock root, burdock root, cayenne
♃	silica	green leafy vegetables, sea vegetables	dandelion root, chicory
♄	calcium	turnip juice, carrot juice, egg yolks, yogurt	comfrey root, comfrey leaf, wintergreen
♅	magnesium, manganese	liquid chlorophyll, leafy green vegetables, whole grains	borage, raspberry leaf, vervain, valerian
♆	potassium, zinc	leafy greens, potatoes, bananas, pumpkin seeds	plantain
♇	E, selenium	wheat germ, cold-pressed oils, kelp, mushrooms	ginseng, dong quai, damiana, squawvine

		TABLE OF ASSOCIATIONS		
Colors	Note	Gems & Crystals	Aromas
gold	B-flat	citrine quartz, amber, topaz, jasper	benzoin, orange (neroli), patchouli
silver	A-flat	moonstone, opal, pearl	cypress, juniper
blue, yellow	F-sharp ♊ C ♍	agate, cat's eye, tiger's eye	cardamom, hyssop, fennel, lavender, rosemary, thyme, peppermint
green, pink	E-flat ♉ D ♎	malachite, emerald, chrysolite, tourmaline, rose quartz	bergamot, rose, jasmine, geranium, ylang-ylang
red	D-flat	bloodstone, ruby, carnelian, garnet	basil, black pepper, cinnamon, ginger
blue-green, yellow (bile)	F	turquoise, chrysocolla	cedarwood, melissa, sandalwood
orange, black	G	diamond, onyx	camphor, eucalyptus, pine
blue	A	lapis lazuli, sapphire, aquamarine	chamomile, marjoram
blue-violet	B	amethyst, jade, fluorite, coral	clary sage, myrrh, frankincense
violet, black	E	smoky quartz, black obsidian, jet, pearl	pennyroyal, sage

In the Beginning— Elements, Qualities, Planets, Signs, and Houses

In the beginning, there was the Earth and the sky, Mother and Father, representing the elements earth and air. There was also water, since much of the Earth's surface was covered by water. Fire was the last of the elements, as fire was made by humans (or as some accounts tell us, a gift from the gods to humans) to represent their spiritual and creative force.

Understanding the **balance of elements** in our individual horoscopes is important; equipped with this knowledge, we can compensate for any imbalances in our individual energy system.

How do we determine this element balance? Older systems of astrology looked to the signs and counted the planets in each sign; they also considered the nodes of the Moon, the Ascendant, and the Midheaven. They spent some time on the houses by element and angular planets. Since the modern discoveries of the asteroids and Chiron and their effect on us, a more complete system is to include Chiron, the planetoid between the orbits of Saturn and Uranus, and the four major asteroids: Ceres, Vesta, Pallas, and Juno. After considering these along with the Sun, Moon, Ascendant, Midheaven, planets, and nodes, it is necessary to look at the planets in terms of the houses in which they fall—fire, earth, air, or water. A predominance in one of the houses or several of the houses of the same element adds a lot of weight to the sign placement.

Next, we consider the planets. Are there any angular planets? (Angular planets are those within five degrees of the Ascendant, Descendant, Midheaven or IC.) Sometimes a person may have little fire in his or her horoscope, but Mars near an angle may make him or her very fiery, or Saturn near an angle would give a strong earth emphasis. For further planetary strength, are any planets conjunct the Sun or Moon? Look to the ruling planet or the planet receiving the most aspects; these factors add extra weight in one's analysis. The outer planets stay in a sign for many years, so the sign placement of Uranus, Neptune, and Pluto would not count for much, whereas the house placement would.

Here is how the signs, houses, and planets break down by element:

Elements: Fire, Earth, Air, and Water

Fire: the signs Aries, Leo, and Sagittarius; the first, fifth, and ninth houses; and Mars, the Sun, and Jupiter; also the planetoid Chiron (the wounded healer with his bow and arrow), which is often associated with Sagittarius.

Earth: the signs Taurus, Virgo, and Capricorn; the second, sixth, and tenth houses; the planet Saturn; and the asteroids Ceres (the Earth Mother and goddess of grain) and Vesta (the vestal virgin and goddess of the hearth). Both of these asteroids represent aspects of Virgo—Ceres, the nurturing Earth energy, and Vesta, the devotion and purity.

Air: the signs Gemini, Libra, and Aquarius; the third, seventh, and eleventh houses; the planets Mercury and Uranus; and the asteroid Pallas. (Pallas Athena is known for her wisdom and mental creativity and is associated with Libra.)

Water: the signs Cancer, Scorpio, and Pisces; the fourth, eighth, and twelfth houses; and the Moon, Neptune, Pluto, and Venus. (Some say Venus is earth and others air because of its dual rulership of Taurus and Libra, and yet Venus has a strongly emotional and aesthetic quality. Aphrodite or Venus rose from the water at birth. Venus probably is a combination of all three elements.) Also, the asteroid Juno, the goddess of marriage traditionally associated with Libra, has come to have a self-sacrificing aspect and an association with Pisces as she was deceived by Zeus many times.

Let's examine the elements in terms of their balance, excess, and lack and see what we can do to work on the extremes of any element.

Fire

Fire stimulates and is creative; with a proper balance of fire, one has good physical energy and vitality and can manifest ideas as action. There is also self-confidence, cheerfulness, optimism, courage, inspiration, warmth, and affection.

The element fire rules the body heat and digestion; it is also related to purification since perspiration enables the body to throw off toxins.

Excess fire can make one angry, hot-tempered, violent, and aggressive. Physiologically, it can cause heartburn, liver problems such as hepatitis, stomach problems such as ulcers, gallbladder problems (excess bile), inflammations, skin eruptions, fevers, and excess perspiration.

To balance excess fire, try cooling foods; swimming and bathing; wearing cool colors as blues and greens; using gemstones as green garnet, aventurine, green calcite, aquamarine, emerald, and malachite; and flower remedies like impatiens for those who are quick to anger or chamomile to calm overly emotional states.

Chinese medicine works with the kidneys, a water organ, to balance excess fire.

Lack of fire causes poor circulation with cold extremities, a stiff body, poor muscle tone, low vitality, indigestion, despondency, lack of courage, and lack of confidence.

For those who lack fire, doing aerobic-type exercises to strengthen the heart and circulatory system is helpful; so are activities like hiking and mountain climbing, which serve to empower people, increasing self-confidence and courage. Add warming spices as cayenne, cinnamon, cardamom, and curry to foods; make herb teas from ginger and peppermint, which stimulate digestion; wear colors as reds and oranges and gemstones like carnelian, ruby, bloodstone, and topaz; try flower remedies as Indian paintbrush and scarlet monkeyflower and aromas as black pepper, basil, and cinnamon.

In Chinese medicine, wood stimulates fire. The liver and gallbladder are organs related to wood, so stimulating these organs is helpful.

Earth

Earth is dense and heavy; those with a balanced earth element are practical, stable, have a sense of responsibility, and can be very caring and nurturing like the Earth herself.

The earth element governs the bones, teeth, skin, cartilage, muscles, tendons, and nails.

Excess earth can manifest as sluggishness, lethargy, a stocky heavy body, a lack of exercise, insensitivity, depression, being overly concerned with material values, a slowness to perceive new ideas, and a crystallization of thoughts and habit patterns.

Exercise of all types can help to balance excess earth. Eating spicy foods and utilizing herbs such as cayenne and ginger can create more fire in the body; fiery colors such as bright yellows and oranges help to energize excess earth types; the crystals carnelian, hematite, rhodochrosite, and fire agates are of benefit; and flower remedies like chestnut bud and chicory break up old patterns, with oak and mustard alleviating depression.

In Chinese medicine, wood controls earth, and stimulating the liver and gallbladder (wood organs) through the acupuncture meridians can help to balance excess earth.

With a lack of earth, individuals do not have the ability to manifest their potential; they may appear unstable, dreamlike, and idealistic.

For those who lack earth, grounding techniques and outdoor exercise are important. Walk barefoot on the Earth Mother to absorb her energy; eat plenty of whole grains and root vegetables like potatoes, squashes, turnips, and beets; utilize the color green and gemstones such as malachite, emerald, chrysoprase, and aventurine; use the flower essences clematis and manzanita for grounding.

In Chinese medicine, fire stimulates earth; utilizing herbs for the heart to stimulate circulation as well as points on the heart and small intestine meridians is helpful.

Air

Air is light and essential for movement; when the air element is balanced, there is grace of physical movement, balanced perception, and good communication with others.

The air element governs the respiratory and nervous systems.

An overabundance of air in the horoscope can make one restless, anxious, nervous, and jittery. Physiologically, this excess can lead to dry rough skin, brittle hair and nails, stiffness of joints as in arthritis, flatulence, asthma, and nervous disorders. Psychologically, too much air can cause one to be detached and impersonal. (Many associate the sign Aquarius with these qualities.)

Air dries up water in the body, so air types tend to be lean in structure; they require a lot of water and liquids as well as oils on the body to balance out the dryness. Outdoor exercise such as walking and swimming is important. Maintain a diet rich in whole grains (which are grounding and contain most of the B complex vitamins) and green leafy vegetables (which contain a lot of chlorophyll, the magnesium ion), supplemented with B complex vitamins, magnesium, and manganese; use deep blue and violet colors to relax the nervous system and crystals such as blue tourmaline, green calcite, and chrysocolla and the gems lapis lazuli, sapphire, and aquamarine to bring mental peace and to balance the nervous system; drink nervine herb teas such as chamomile, catnip, scullcap, vervain, hops, and valerian; try flower remedies such as white chestnut, mimulus, morning glory, and lavender.

In Chinese medicine, fire controls air, so hot spicy foods that promote circulation and digestion are helpful.

Lack of air may lead to difficulties in perception, introversion, tiredness, shortness of breath, and slowness of movement.

For those who lack air, deep breathing exercises are a necessity. Work with groups to enhance communications skills; try dancing and becoming aware of movement through space. Herb teas such as gotu kola and fo ti (Chinese herb called the "elixir of life") stimulate brain activity; flower remedies such as scleranthus, sweet pea, quaking grass, and penstemon help one relate to groups.

In Chinese medicine, earth stimulates air; working with the stomach and spleen meridians would therefore be advisable.

Water

Water is cleansing and flowing; when it is balanced, an individual can relate emotionally to others and have proper empathy without becoming too subjective. Those with a preponderance of the water element are in touch with their intuitive faculties and can manifest creative abilities. Water softens and rounds out the body and gives it smoothness and gentleness.

Physiologically, water rules the lymphatic system and all the fluids in the body, such as the blood and various secretions.

Excess water in the horoscope may cause one to be overweight, drowsy, self-indulgent, dreamy, and security conscious. It may manifest in physical conditions such as mucus accumulation, colds, and lymphatic congestion.

To balance excess water, one should eat mostly cooked foods and some spicy foods; drink diuretic herb teas such as dandelion leaf, nettles, and alfalfa; and try flower remedies such as honeysuckle, red chestnut, chamomile, clematis, and pink yarrow for emotional sensitivity and psychic protection. The crystals rose quartz, kunzite, pink tourmaline, and green aventurine are soothing and healing for the emotions, while amethyst, fluorite, and sugilite work with the emotions on a higher plane.

In Chinese medicine, the earth element (stomach and spleen) controls water, so working with these organs through acupuncture or acupressure may be helpful.

Those who lack water are unable to show their feelings or express their empathy; their bodies lack smoothness and they often suffer from thirst and dehydration.

To balance this lack, one should drink more fluids like vegetable juices and herb teas; live near the water; take classes in the arts as a way of expressing the intuitive and creative side of nature; use the flower remedies holly, sticky monkeyflower, fuchsia, garlic, and Black-Eyed Susan to release and express emotions; and wear the gemstones pearl, tourmaline, and opal to inspire creativity, as well as smoky quartz and black obsidian to release old emotions.

In Chinese medicine, air stimulates water; this is done through working with the lung and large intestine meridians.

Qualities: The Cardinal, Fixed, and Mutable Crosses

In addition to analyzing the horoscope for elements, the qualities of cardinal, fixed, and mutable are also important. Besides counting the number of planets (as well as Chiron and the four asteroids, the Ascendant and the Midheaven) in cardinal, fixed, and mutable signs, it is important to look at the angular, succedent, and cadent houses to see how many planets and asteroids are in each.

The **cardinal** signs are the signs that begin each season: Aries and Libra, the equinoxes, and Cancer and Capricorn, the solstices. They correspond to the **angular** houses: the first, fourth, seventh, and tenth. Cardinal energy is one of action, duty, and responsibility. Those who have an emphasis of cardinal planets or planets in angular houses tend to solve their problems through outward action and relationships rather than through inner scrutiny of psychological motives or by adapting to outward circumstances. Cardinal emphasis leads to initiation of new projects, being out in the world; it is energetic and aggressive. Aries, the "I," is balanced by Libra, the "we." Individual desires must be balanced by considering the greater whole or relationships. Cancer represents personal security and home, while Capricorn needs to be out in the world, accepting responsibilities, organizing new projects, and teaching.

For those who have an excess of planets in the cardinal signs and angular houses, meditation and reflection is important. Practice physical disciplines such as yoga and tai chi that focus on inner awareness; use crystals such as amethyst, fluorite, and sugilite to work on developing the higher centers. Those lacking cardinal emphasis need to get out in the world and become active; the martial arts, particularly aikido, can stimulate their energy; crystals and gems such as carnelian, jasper, hematite, rhodochrosite, ruby, and blood-stone will also help.

The **fixed** cross represents those time periods on the Earth Mother when we experience intensely the energy of each season: Taurus—spring, Leo—summer, Scorpio—fall, and Aquarius—winter. They correspond to the **succedent** houses: the second, fifth, eighth, and eleventh. Fixed sign energy tends to be stable and dependable; its negative qualities are becoming stubborn, tenacious, and resisting change. Taurus is willful and can become attached to possessions and value systems, but Scorpio can help to transform these tenden-cies, unless one gets stuck in a sense of power or their desire nature. Leo likes to be domineering and manipulate people, but can learn through Aquarius to be a humanitarian and let go of the ego, unless one becomes set in reforming society and others. Fixed signs work slower than others, are more introverted and self-sufficient, and are less likely to work within relationships.

Those with an excess of energy in the fixed modality often need deep body therapies such as rolfing and bioenergetics to break up old physical and emo-tional patterns and flower essences such as chicory, chestnut bud, fuchsia, Black-Eyed Susan, and trillium. Crystals like smoky quartz and black obsidian are often beneficial. Those lacking fixed energy need physical disciplines that provide grounding, such as outdoor walks or running; they need to work on strengthening their will and on following through with projects. Crystals like tiger's-eye and hawk's-eye help ground higher energies into the body; foods such as grains and root vegetables are also helpful.

The **mutable** cross occurs at those times of the year when the seasonal energy is changing: Gemini—late spring; Virgo—late summer; Sagittarius—late fall; and Pisces—late winter, corresponding to the **cadent** houses. Those with dominant mutable sign and cadent house emphasis tend to be more flexible and adaptable; they can also be more scattered, undisciplined, and wishy-washy. Gemini can put energy into too many projects and become easily distracted, while Sagittarius can become overextended and travel to too many places. Virgo can get caught up with details and overanalysis, while Pisces can tend to be unrealistic and a daydreamer. All the mutable signs need to learn focus and discipline of energies. With balance, a mutable emphasis can readily analyze and disseminate new information.

Excess mutable emphasis needs grounding and focusing. The physical disciplines yoga, tai chi, and the martial arts are helpful; flower remedies such as white chestnut, madia, shasta daisy, vervain, and wild oat can work to focus and integrate energies; the crystals and gemstones green calcite, aventurine, chrysoprase, chrysocolla, and malachite ground energy. Lack of mutable emphasis can make one rigid and crystallized in attitudes. Flowing movements as in dance and tai chi are helpful to the body; flower essences like rock water, quaking grass, and willow, as well as crystals like rose quartz, kunzite, and sugilite may be needed.

Planets

☉ SUN—Leo

The symbol of the Sun is a circle with a dot in the center, representing the vitality and ego of each being. The Sun radiates light and power as each individual radiates out from the core center or nucleus. Just as the Sun is in the center of the galaxy, so the Sun in the astrological chart represents the essence or center of one's being. It also stands for any male figure as father, husband, or other figures of authority. It represents the true self or will.

In the body, the Sun rules the heart or the cardiovascular system, which gives life to the rest of the cells.

☽ MOON—Cancer

The Moon, which reflects the light of the Sun, is ever changing and reflective. The Moon is feminine and often referred to as Grandmother Moon in many societies. She represents the unconscious side of the personality, the instincts and desires. As we strive to fulfill our ego needs represented by the Sun, we are still bound by our instincts and habit patterns, our more unconscious lunar side. Whereas the Sun is a unity, the Moon is dual and its symbol suggests two horns. The Moon waxes and wanes, symbolizing the dual process of death and rebirth.

In the body the Moon rules the fluids, the secretions of the glands and digestive juices, and the mucous membranes.

☿ MERCURY—Gemini and Virgo

Mercury, or Hermes, the winged messenger, is a link between the Sun and the Moon. Mercury is the playful child who goes back and forth, communicating and analyzing material. Its symbol is threefold. The cross of matter beneath represents the practical world; the solar symbol above, the spirit; and the horns of the Moon surmount it. This symbol shows that the intellect reflects the changing quality of the Moon. In the astrological horoscope, the placement of Mercury shows how an individual communicates and how one classifies effects that impinge upon the senses.

In the body, Mercury rules the nervous system, which sends impulses to every cell of the body. Mercury also rules the respiratory system and the functions of speech and hearing.

♀ VENUS—Taurus and Libra

Venus, the goddess of beauty, is the Earth's next-door neighbor. It is through Venus we must travel (the principle of love) to get to the Sun, or center of any matter. Thus, our purpose here on Earth is to understand Venus and to employ our Venusian creative talents if we are to get to the heart of any issue. Venus' desire for harmony sublimates the sexual drive into socially acceptable modes of relating (the Libran function). Venus also represents the Earth Mother with her ripeness and profusion of sensuality (the Taurean aspect). Color, music, sound—all the senses are ruled by Venus and enable us to live our life here on Earth with adornment and beauty.

In the body, Venus rules the throat and thyroid gland, kidneys, and bladder.

♂ MARS—Aries

Mars, the warrior and aggressor, stands on the other side of the Earth from Venus. The glyph for Mars shows the cross of matter over the circle of spirit. This cross is in the form of an arrow, representing the passions and desires. This is the same arrow represented in the glyph of Scorpio of which Mars is co-ruler. Whereas Venus represents love and harmony and spirit rising above material limitations, Mars shows the spirit held down by the weight of the cross. Our Earth walk is to balance these two polar forces.

Physiologically, Mars rules the blood, muscles, and adrenal glands. Conditions arising from overheating, such as fevers, infections, and redness, are under the rulership of Mars as well.

♃ JUPITER—Sagittarius

Jupiter, or Zeus, is the king of the gods and the largest planet. He is the great benefactor representing the principle of growth and expansion upon Earth. The glyph of Jupiter shows the crescent Moon turned outward alongside the cross. According to the myth, Jupiter was raised on the milk of a goat whose horns overflowed with food and drink. This was the origin of the horn of plenty. Jupiter represents the social order that determines behavior and morals. Jupiter bestows the gift of prophecy and an optimistic faith. He stimulates us to look beyond the names and forms of things to understand their philosophical implications.

Physiologically, Jupiter rules the liver and pancreas and the sciatic nerve (the largest nerve in the body). Conditions of excess growth like tumors and obesity are also ruled by Jupiter.

♄ SATURN—Capricorn

Saturn, or Cronus, was the oldest god—he was the timekeeper and lawgiver as well as the taskmaster of those on Earth. Saturn has always been regarded as a teacher and tester; he represents perfect justice and highest achievement; he solidifies and grounds energy by relating it to the Earth and practical matters. It is Saturn that provides the structure for the minerals and rocks on the Earth. Saturn can also be cold and constricting, shutting out the rays of the Sun from Earth's children when they feel bound by duty or obligation. The glyph for Saturn is composed of the same cross and crescent as the glyph for Jupiter, but here the cross of matter is on top, showing the material responsibilities that strong Saturn individuals feel.

Saturn governs the body structure, the backbone, the teeth, bones, joints, nails, and skin.

♅ URANUS—Aquarius

Uranus, the awakener of humanity to a new age, has the most eccentric orbit among the planets. Uranus spins in a different way from the others, lying on its side and rolling about its orbit. Uranus stands for anything that is unconventional, rebellious, individualistic. It rules electricity and atomic radiation (first released through the agency of the element uranium). Intuitive insight comes in flashes, and as a higher octave of Mercury, Uranus goes beyond the boundaries of Saturn to break up old patterns and structures. The glyph for Uranus derives from the letter H (for William Herschel, who discovered the planet); it is two half crescents separated by the cross of matter.

As a higher octave of Mercury, Uranus is related to the nervous system; it governs the electrical force that flows through the nerve channels. Spasm, cramps, and irregular heartbeat are all ruled by Uranus.

♆ NEPTUNE—Pisces

Neptune, or Poseidon, the sea god, brings water to Mother Earth and flows through each individual as the potential to attune to cosmic consciousness and a transcendent reality. Neptune is the higher octave of Venus, bringing the Venusian love to the level of compassion and mysticism. Its positive vibration brings forth music, poetry, dance, film, and photography; its negative vibration causes Earth beings to escape through fantasy, drugs, alcohol, and other Neptunian illusions. The glyph for Neptune is the trident, which is comprised of the chalice of the Moon, the receptive principle, superimposed over the cross of matter. Thus, Neptune shows how material reality can be transcended into states of higher consciousness.

Physiologically, Neptune rules the cerebrospinal fluid, the pineal gland, and the lymphatic system. It governs obscure diseases that are difficult to diagnose, as well as alcoholism, addiction, and those characterized by the spirit disconnecting from the body, such as hallucinations, schizophrenia, and other psychoses.

♇ or ♀ PLUTO—Scorpio

Pluto, or Hades, was the god of the underworld and was feared by earthlings. Pluto spent half his time above ground and half below ground and thus was able to perceive the lower depths or subconscious mind. Pluto leads Earth beings through processes of death, rebirth, and purification, just as the seasons change and dark becomes light. Pluto is a higher octave of Mars, and when its power bursts forth, it is a volcano erupting. (Mars may be compared to a bomb exploding.) One glyph for Pluto is comprised of the letters PL, which stands for Pluto and the Lowell observatory where Pluto was discovered. The other glyph has the cross of matter under the chalice or half-circle of the Moon with the full circle on top. This full circle is the Sun or spiritual principle that emerges as a result of the transformation experienced through Pluto's energy.

Pluto rules the reproductive system and the excretory system, including the colon and anus. It relates to hidden cell changes and destruction of tissue.

Asteroids

The asteroid belt is located between Mars and Jupiter; the four largest asteroids—Ceres, Vesta, Juno, and Pallas—are used in astrological interpretation and provide additional insights into the horoscope.

⚲ CERES—Virgo and Cancer

Ceres, or Demeter, as she was known to the Greeks (from *da mater* meaning "the mother"), was the Great Mother or Earth Mother, the goddess of grain and fertility. She was the mother of Persephone–Kore who was abducted by Pluto (Hades) to the underworld where she spent part of each year. Ceres' search and reunion with her daughter formed the basis for the Eleusinian mysteries, which were celebrated in Greece for thousands of years. In her role as goddess of grain and agriculture, Ceres is associated with the sign Virgo and has the quality of hard work as well as representing the harvest time of the year. As the nurturing and protective mother, Ceres is associated with the sign Cancer and along with the Moon rules child-bearing and fertility.

In the horoscope, those having Ceres prominent are often healers and may be doctors, nurses, massage therapists, nutritional consultants, or may care for many people. When Ceres comes to the Sun, Moon, Ascendant, Venus or Mars by progression or transit, it may be a time for childbearing or some work connected with children or nurturing. The glyph of Ceres is the sickle used in agriculture.

In the body, Ceres is related to the fertility cycle for women (as is Juno); a prominent Ceres often may indicate strong healing and nurturing tendencies.

⚶ VESTA—Virgo and Scorpio

Vesta, or Hestia, was the goddess of the hearth, a symbol of protection and keeper of the sacred fire. She was also one of the vestal virgins who were known for their purity and devotion. The vestal virgins were not literally virgins; they simply were not involved in sexual relationships for personal or procreative reasons, but, as vehicles of the kundalini fire and as representations of the Goddess, had sexual encounters with men who came to the temples to worship. Their sexuality then was connected with their religion, and personal expression of sexuality was sublimated to reach union with the divine and the cosmic self. Vesta is therefore associated with Virgo's devotion, purity, and sexual abstinence, and with Scorpio as the symbol of kundalini energy and transformation of sexuality to an impersonal level.

A prominent Vesta in the natal horoscope indicates one who is hard-working but also has a strong devotional and mystical side. It may signify one who spends more time alone than in relationships, committed to inner work. Transits from Vesta often signify a time to withdraw from relationships and spend time alone or in a monastic setting. The glyph of Vesta represents the sacred hearth with the fires above.

Physiologically, Vesta is related to problems with the sexual or reproductive organs.

⚵ JUNO—Libra and Scorpio

Juno, or Hera (the Greek *he era* means "the earth"), was the goddess of marriage and also governed the female reproductive cycle. Juno suffered much through Zeus' infidelity and expressed her rage at the women involved. On the one hand, Juno epitomizes the "Hierogamos" or Sacred Marriage because she gives up her career, social life, and beliefs for a committed relationship. In this way, she is associated with the sign Libra. On the other hand, Juno experiences jealousy and possessiveness and acts vindictively. These qualities are associated with Scorpio. Juno also uses sexuality to transcend her personal identity by committing herself to a relationship. She symbolizes a union that is emotionally and sexually fulfilling while also symbolizing the sacrifices that are made for marriage and the abuse of women by men. The aspects to Juno in the horoscope may shed some light on how committed relationships work in the life—whether it is possible to have relationships and retain one's individuality, or whether one loses oneself through the union. In a woman's horoscope, Juno may also refer to the sacrificial qualities of the feminine and abuse by men. The glyph of Juno is the scepter of royalty.

As ruler of the female reproductive cycle, Juno is often prominent by transit when a woman conceives a child. There may be other relationships to the reproductive cycle, but those have not been researched as of this writing.

♀ PALLAS ATHENA—Libra and Aquarius

Pallas Athena was the virgin goddess of wisdom who ruled the city of Athens. She was the goddess of war and is always pictured wearing her armor; she also rules the visual arts, the crafts, and as Hygeia, she was the goddess of health and healing. Being born from the head of Zeus, Athena symbolized the ascent of the patriarchal culture and the demise of the matriarchy. She was her father's daughter and never acknowledged her mother Metis. Basically, she portrays the independent, aggressive, and competitive woman. Astrologically, Pallas is related to the sign Libra and to Aquarius. Her rulership of the arts and crafts like weaving, pottery, and embroidery relate to Libra; her transpersonal social concerns, capacity for inspired vision, and emotional aloofness are typical of Aquarius.

A prominent Pallas suggests an involvement in social causes, counseling, and healing, with possible work in the arts, depending on the rest of the horoscope. For women, a prominent Pallas may also portray the competitive, aggressive spirit in business and a strong independence. The glyph for Pallas is her spear.

Stressful aspects to Pallas may indicate poor vision, color blindness, and dyslexia.

⚷ CHIRON—Sagittarius and Virgo

Chiron, first thought to be a planetoid and later a comet, orbits between Saturn and Uranus. Chiron (from the Greek root meaning "hand" and the source of such words as *chiropody*, *chirognomy*, and *chiropractic*) was the wounded healer in mythology, and synchronous with its discovery was the burgeoning holistic health movement with its emphasis on healing with the hands.

Chiron was born of an illicit union between Cronus (Saturn), who took the form of a horse, and Philyra, a sea nymph. Chiron thus had the lower portions of a horse and the upper torso and head of a man. The birth took place in a cave where Chiron continued to live and taught many of the Greek heroes. He taught Asklepios the art of healing through herbs and surgery; he also taught astrology to Hercules, according to one legend. Asklepios brought together astrology with parts of the body and their diseases, as well as timing for days of illness. This knowledge was later amplified by Hippocrates, the father of modern medicine.

Compared to the planets, Chiron has an elliptical and eccentric path; it crosses Saturn's orbit at perihelion (closest to the Sun) and even gets nearer to us than Saturn, and at aphelion (furthest from the Sun) it touches Uranus' orbit. It has therefore been termed the bridge between these two and a significant planetary body for the new age in that it points the way to the transformation of Saturnian modes of thinking, which tend to be rational and structured, into highly intuitive and inspirational Uranian modes.

Chiron's death points out some interesting teachings for our time. Chiron sustained a wound from one of Hercules' poisoned arrows that accidentally pierced his ankle. He continued to suffer because of his immortality and thus offered his life in place of Prometheus, who was chained in the underworld as punishment for stealing fire from the gods and bringing it to humans. Chiron showed great compassion for Prometheus, and embraced his own death willingly. Zeus placed him in the sky as the constellation Sagittarius, the archer with his bow. Chiron's association with Sagittarius stems from this fact, and his association with Virgo derives from his extraordinary gifts of healing and his service to humans while alive. Chiron has been associated with Scorpio (the glyph of Scorpio also has an arrow) due to the way he died and his teachings regarding healing. Basically, he is allied with the fire element as he truly symbolizes the impassioned Jupiterian teacher who understands his own power and is able to be a catalyst in giving fire back to humanity.

Chiron is prominent in the horoscopes of healers and those who undergo a strong healing crisis themselves, which is often their initiation into the healing field. Many doctors, nurses, therapists, herbalists, acupuncturists, chiropractors, as well as those who work with crystals and subtle forms of healing, have Chiron conjunct one of the angles, the Sun or the Moon.

Physiologically, Chiron transits relate to times in the life where there may be serious health crises, or when strong cleansing and healing therapies are most effective.

The Aspects

Looking at the aspects between planets is important in determining where the imbalances are and what areas of the body and psyche are receiving more stress.

Hard aspects are considered the most important in the work of healing with the horoscope. These are the conjunction (two planets next to each other), the opposition (180 degrees), the square (90 degrees), the semisquare (45 degrees), and the sesquiquadrate (135 degrees). All of these aspects are action-oriented and are based on the division of the circle by one, two, four, and eight, respectively. The opposition, square, semisquare, and sesquiquadrate may cause friction or tension. Another important aspect is the inconjunct or quincunx (150 degrees). This aspect represents the distance from the first to the sixth house and is characterized by the word *adjustment*. It is used in Medical Astrology as it often manifests physiologically.

Soft aspects are based on the division of the circle by three, six, and twelve. The trine (120 degrees), sextile (60 degrees), and semisextile (30 degrees) bring ease and harmony. Suggested orbs are 6 degrees for the conjunction, opposition, square, and trine; 3 degrees for the sextile, inconjunct, sesquiquadrate, and semisquare; 1 degree for a semisextile.

Minor aspects include the quintile (72 degrees) and biquintile (144 degrees), which are a division of the circle by five; the septile (51.26 degrees) and biseptile (104 degrees), a division of the circle by seven; and the nonagen (40 degrees), a division of the circle by nine. These aspects work more on a subtle and spiritual level; using too many aspects could become confusing in a chart analysis.

Having both hard and soft aspects to major planets is important for balance. With a preponderance of hard aspects and lack of soft aspects, healing can become difficult at times and extremely challenging. When there are mostly soft aspects and few hard aspects, one may tend to lack motivation.

Parallels and Contraparallels

Declination is the distance a planet is placed north or south of the celestial equator. (The range of possible declinations is only 26 degrees North or South.) If two planets are in the same declination (with a one degree orb), they are considered parallel; if one is North and the other South (with a one degree orb), they are considered contraparallel. A parallel is like a conjunction, and a contraparallel is like an opposition. Often additional information will be gathered if the parallels are included. Mars contraparallel Neptune may indicate a weak immune system even if there are no major aspects between the two planets in the horoscope.

The Twelve Signs

♈ ARIES

Aries symbolizes springtime, when flowers and trees burst into bloom. It is the initiator of action and processes on the Earth. All new beginnings are governed by Aries; ruled by the planet Mars, it is related to aggressive, impulsive actions. Individuals with the Sun, Moon, Ascendant, or several planets in Aries can be headstrong and impulsive as they plunge into situations and projects without being aware of their consequences and without completing them.

The glyph of Aries is the Ram's horn. The time of the year represented by Aries was the time when the ram was at rest after breeding with the ewes. The Egyptians pictured him resting; the Babylonians and Sumerians referred to this constellation as "the hired laborer" because it was the time when they prepared their fields for sowing. The Greeks identified Aries with the Golden Fleece, which was guarded day and night by a dragon until it was rescued by Jason. During the age of Aries (2160 B.C.–0 C.E.), the ram was used as a religious sacrifice; his death marked a rebirth, the ending and beginning of a cycle of life.

Aries rules the head and the brain area; it is related to the process of respiration where we take in oxygen and let out carbon dioxide. Many Arian individuals have problems with headaches and migraines as a result of tension in the head area.

♉ TAURUS

If the ram is battering and impulsive, the bull that follows is slow, steady, and stubborn. Where Aries plants the seed, Taurus takes it and roots it firmly into the ground. Taurus governs money and possessions and the values these represent. Ruled by the planet Venus, Taureans have a taste for beautiful objects and clothes. Unlike the passionate Arians, Taureans have a steadier and more sensual love nature. Taurus is an extremely fertile sign—it represents the time of year when seeds and sprouts are flowering and the lushness of Mother Nature abounds. Those with a strong Taurus influence are often obstinate or bull-necked, but they can be loving and persevering and may bend their necks willingly. An unevolved Taurean can often become a "bully." Taurus takes the resources from Aries, accumulates them and makes them grow. In the financial world, "a bull market" reflects growth and prosperity.

Taurus is a Roman word that derived from the Greek *tau*. *Tau* (a prototype of our T) was a pictogram for sexual intercourse, the short bar on top representing the female vulva, and the long bar, the male phallus. The symbol implied the origin of life and its continuity.

The cow or bull was venerated as a fertility symbol in many cultures and used as a religious symbol in the Paleolithic period. Likenesses of bulls guarded temple gates, and their horns were mounted on temple shrines. Bulls were sacrificed during the Spring Equinox so that their blood might quicken the life stirring within the Earth. The cult of the bull in ancient Egypt was centered on a living animal, the bull Apis, held to be the earthly representative of the god Apis who lived in the underworld. Each bull was selected by distinctive markings representing the four fixed signs of the zodiac: Leo, Aquarius, Taurus and Scorpio. This sacred bull was the center of orthodox religious ceremonies; during his lifetime, he was worshipped and treated with deepest reverence. When he died, there was a period of mourning throughout the country. The minotaur, half man and half bull, was the national deity of Crete. There were also the human-faced winged bulls from Nineveh, and in the age of Taurus (4320 B.C.–2160 B.C.), Britain was known as the "Sacred Island of the White Bull," whose cult must have been widespread as it gave rise to the national prototype, or "John Bull."

In the body, Taurus rules the neck and throat. Taurean natives often have problems with the thyroid gland, located in the throat area. This is due to their holding back and not expressing their love and creative energy.

♊ GEMINI

Gemini is a mutable, adaptable sign, representing the Twins Castor and Pollux in the sky. Gemini disseminates the information and resources accumulated by Taurus. As an air sign, Gemini represents the hot dry time of late spring and early summer when the air is fragrant with the plants and blossoms of spring.

The symbol of the sign Gemini consists of two upright lines between two horizontal lines, an arrangement that suggests the doorposts and lintel. The Ancient Twins were the guardians of all doors and entrances. They were identified with the sacred pillars of Jachin and Boaz at Jerusalem and frequently found at the gates of Babylonian, Assyrian, and Egyptian temples. Two pillars were also associated with the mysteries of Eleusis. From early times, the island of Samothrace was dedicated to the cult of the twins. Here the aboriginal people of Greece celebrated the mysteries of Cabeiri or the Great Ones consisting of a Mother Goddess and her two children. Many centuries later these twin deities were known to the Romans as Castor and Pollux. According to the legend, one of these was divine and one was human. Castor and Pollux were known as the Dioscuri, the sons of Zeus. When the mortal Castor was killed, Zeus, in answer to the prayer of the immortal Pollux, transported them to the heaven world where they shine as the constellation of Gemini. During the age of Gemini (6840 B.C.–4320 B.C.), many alphabets and forms of script originated.

As Gemini is ruled by the winged messenger Mercury, those with a strong Gemini influence involve themselves with communication and writing skills. They are usually extremely versatile as seen in the dual nature of the sign. Often they spread themselves too thin and flit from one thing to another. The evolved Geminian, however, has the ability to focus and combine the energies of Heaven and Earth represented by the two pillars. In doing this, Gemini becomes a cosmic networker connecting people and ideas all over the world.

Gemini rules the two lungs as well as the arms. Gemini natives often have problems with breathing and respiratory disease, especially when they forget to balance their energies and spend too much time in the mental realm.

⊗ CANCER

Cancer the Crab is another cardinal point of the zodiac, representing the Summer Solstice, the beginnings of hot days balanced by the cool nurturing waters of Cancer. At this time the Sun reaches its highest point in northern declination and then retreats backwards, crablike, to the ecliptic. Cancer is ruled by the Moon and its receptive water principle. The Egyptians depicted this sign by a scarab, which was also a creature of the Moon due to its protective efforts.

Throughout history, the Moon has been worshipped as the personification of the divine feminine force. As the Moon, the Goddess brought many gifts, the most precious being light in the midst of darkness, equated with wisdom and insight. The Great Mother Goddess and her many cults came into being during the age of Cancer (8640 B.C.–6480 B.C.). In ancient Egypt she was known as Isis, goddess of the Moon and Magic; in Crete, she was worshipped as "Our Lady of the Mountain and the Moon"; in Chaldea, as Nana, the goddess of creation, fertility, and abundance; in Greece, as Artemis Cybele; and in Rome, as Rhea, suckling the twins Romulus and Remus. In China and Japan, the worship of the Great Mother is still evident in the sanctity of the home and in ancestor worship.

As the Primal Mother, the Moon also imparts her cycle to humans. The 28-day cycle of the Moon is a woman's menstrual cycle, and her moods and physiological changes during the cycle correspond to the phases of the Moon. Water was another factor connecting the Moon and women. The Moon affects tides, and all the waters on Earth were said to be from the womb of the Moon, just as the individual fetus is cradled in water.

Like the crab, Cancer people can be extremely outgoing or retreat into their shell when they feel vulnerable. Since they are so emotionally sensitive, they need to learn how to protect themselves without withdrawing. They are nurturing and giving, tending to emotional insecurity due to their very sensitive nature.

Physiologically, Cancer rules the breasts, the stomach, the fluids in the body such as the sac surrounding the heart and the sac around the eyes, and all protective places. When they are particularly vulnerable, Cancer people may develop problems in these areas of the body; when they hold back their emotions, they tend to retain fluids.

♌ LEO

Leo the Lion is a fixed fire sign ruled by the Sun, indicating that the Sun is at its hottest when the time of Leo is at hand. The lion is the king of the beasts and has been used as a mystical symbol throughout the ages. In the ancient mysteries, the lion denoted the fearlessness of one who was imbued with Divine Truth. Candidates who successfully passed the ancient Mithraic initiations were called "lions" and were marked upon their foreheads with the Egyptian cross. Mithra himself is often pictured with the head of a lion and two pairs of wings. The reference to the lion and the "gift of the lion's paw" in the Master Mason's degree may have originated from the Mithraic cult. The Sun rising over the back of the lion has always been considered symbolic of power and rulership. The Egyptian priests wore the skins of lions in many of their ceremonies. In ancient days, the corona of the Sun was shown in the form of a lion's mane, a reminder of the fact that at one time the Summer Solstice took place in the sign of the lion. Initiates of the Egyptian mysteries were sometimes called lions or panthers.

The lion was the emissary of the Sun, symbolizing light, truth, and regeneration. The figure of a lion placed on either side of doors and gateways is an emblem of divine guardianship. As the lion symbolizes secret wisdom, to overcome this beast was to master such wisdom. Both Samson and Hercules conquered the lion; there is also the biblical story of Daniel in the lion's den. The lion with the bull, eagle, and man represent the four comers of creation (each associated with one of the fixed signs of the zodiac—Taurus, Leo, Scorpio, and Aquarius). Biblical kings from the line of Judah were referred to as the "lion of Judah."

Sun worship was an age-old religious tradition. Many people date their history as a race or nation from the appearance of a Divine Being who was descended from the Sun and reigned on Earth as a regent for the Father in Heaven. Osiris in Egypt, Apollo, Hermes, and Dionysus in Greece, and Abraham as patriarch of the Hebraic tribes were such figures. They founded a royal line whose members were the guardians of a secret wisdom. These were all prominent during the age of Leo (10,800 B.C.–8640 B.C.). Sun worship is the oldest and purest form of monotheism. People prayed to the Sun and tended a sacred fire, which was extinguished and rekindled at the Winter Solstice. This ceremony symbolized the rebirth of the Sun.

The native of the sign Leo likes to be "lionized" by admirers; the sign represents strong individuality and will. Like a king, Leo enjoys ruling over subjects. A group of lions is called a "pride," and pride is also one of Leo's strongest traits. Evolved Leo types are generous, magnanimous, and courageous. (The word *courageous* comes from the Latin *cor*, meaning "heart.") It is important for Leo natives to be masters of their own instincts and desires.

As the Sun is the heart (core) of the solar system, Leo rules the heart and circulatory system. When Leonians block their love and generosity, they often develop heart and circulatory problems.

♍ VIRGO

Virgo, the sign of service and health, begins the harvest season when the fruits of the Earth are gathered. This is a busy time of the year, and it symbolizes the diligence of the Virgoan worker. The glyph for Virgo is like that of Scorpio, but the M has a closed side, which stands for the female generative organs in the virgin state. Virgo is symbolized by a picture of a maiden carrying a sheaf of wheat to show that Virgoans understand the principle of discrimination in separating the wheat from the chaff.

The Earth goddess was common to all cultures. In Egypt, Isis–Hathor represented the Earth and its feminine power. She was called Ceres (from which we get the word *cereal*) by the Romans and Demeter by the Greeks. During the lunar month of Virgo, the Egyptians planted flowers and harvested corn. The signal for the harvest to begin was the appearance, at moonrise, of the star Spica, or "ear of corn." In North America, prayers are sent to the Corn Mother or the Three Sisters—maize, beans, and squash.

Virgo is ruled by Mercury, which shows the strong mental quality of the sign. Virgoans tend to submit all matters to meticulous analysis. On the negative, this can manifest as being overly critical and judgmental. The positive side of Virgo, however, is its ability to discriminate, its careful attention to detail, and its service and concern with health and healing.

Physiologically, Virgo rules the digestive tract, specifically the small intestine. Many individuals with a strong Virgo emphasis tend to have problems with digestion and assimilation. This is because they are often going too fast or being overly mental and not assimilating experiences in their own lives.

♎ LIBRA

Libra, the sign of Balance, the only zodiacal sign that does not have something animate as its symbol, represents the Fall Equinox, a time when day and night are equal. This symbol was added to the zodiac at a much later time. It comes from Egypt by way of ancient Rome. The Egyptian glyph stood for the month when the harvest was weighed prior to selling it or storing it. The Romans interpreted this glyph as related to law or legal concerns. Originally, the sign Libra was "Chonsu the child," the "traveler of the night skies." He had the symbol of the New Moon on his head and was the son of the Great Goddess. He became the symbol for the Earth's yield, the ripened crops ready for harvesting. Later, two youths were represented, one for the waxing half of the year, one for the waning half, thus giving Libra its dual quality.

Libra governs relationships and partnerships; it involves balancing "I" with "We." Unlike Leo, who will settle for love affairs, Libra needs to make its liaisons formal with rituals and legal contracts. Libra refers to the laws of justice as well as those of harmony and proportion. Libran natives have a strong sensitivity to aesthetics and are often involved in painting, music, or some other art form.

Anatomically, Libra rules the kidneys and bladder, which regulate the liquid contents of the body and eliminate waste products. If one is not clear in relationships and not eliminating emotional patterns, problems in these areas may develop.

♏ SCORPIO

Scorpio's symbol is similar to Virgo's except that it has an arrow pointing upward referring to the sexual energy associated with the sign. Scorpio, ruled by Pluto, is linked with autumn, the dying part of the year, and thus has come to represent the death and rebirth process in human beings and their psychological transformations as they evolve through their many changes.

Scorpio's symbols, the scorpion, the snake, and the eagle, are bound up with matters of life and death. The Egyptians saw the constellation Scorpio as Selqet, the scorpion goddess who released her hordes of scorpions during Egypt's annual sandstorms. They watched its position in the sky in order to prepare and protect themselves. They named these stars the serpent stars. Snakes have always been a mystical and religious symbol, dating back to the Garden of Eden in Genesis. Their appeal is their ability to cast off their old skins and come into new ones, just as the Earth renews herself each season. The eagle has always been a symbol of regeneration; in Native American symbolism he stands for the East, the beginning of a new day and new directions.

Scorpio natives have the ability to probe matters deeply and to act as catalysts for growth and change in others. When they are vibrating at the lower octave of Scorpio, they may sting like the scorpion. At the higher octave, they can transcend their jealousy and nastiness and soar like the eagle. Scorpio also represents sexuality in its role as a transformative process. Eastern religious and philosophical literature abounds in descriptions of the awakening of the kundalini energy (the dormant snake at the root of the spine). Whereas Scorpio natives have the ability to transform outworn behavioral patterns, they are also good managers of other people's money and finances. Scorpio rules investments, inheritances, and the resources and values of others, whereas its opposite, Taurus, refers to individual resources and values.

Physiologically, Scorpio rules the reproductive system and the organs of elimination like the colon, anus, and rectum. Those individuals who hold back their emotions and don't eliminate old patterns tend to have problems in these areas.

♐ SAGITTARIUS

At the time of Sagittarius, the night force gets stronger, outlasting the day force, and one's mind turns inward to religious and philosophical pursuits. Travel, sports, and games may engage those less intellectually minded. The glyph of Sagittarius is the arrow of the Archer with a piece of the bow. The sign is said to represent Chiron the centaur who was educated by Artemis and Apollo and became a teacher of Achilles, Asklepios, and other Greek heroes. However, Hercules shot him with a poisoned arrow, and his pain was so excruciating that he chose to die and trade his immortality for Prometheus' mortality, releasing Prometheus from the punishment of being chained to a rock while vultures picked at his liver.

The goddess Artemis or Diana, the Amazon warrior huntress, is also associated with this sign. She represents the woman who proved her strength and athletic prowess in order to be a Moon priestess. Thus, the association of both physical strength and inner wisdom in the sign Sagittarius is understood.

Sagittarius is both a teacher and a preacher. As a teacher, Sagittarius represents the virtues of devotion to truth, pursuit of knowledge, and maintenance of high moral standards. As a preacher, Sagittarius may tend to proselytize, because of acquired knowledge and wisdom. Unlike Scorpions who keep their knowledge hidden until they are sure of it, Sagittarians like to share their visions and ideas. They tend to be excessive when it comes to eating and drinking and overly optimistic with regard to speculative matters like horse racing and gambling.

Sagittarius is ruled by the planet Jupiter, which governs the liver and pancreas. Often Sagittarians tend to have a weakness in these organs from overindulging. Sagittarius also rules the thighs, which are our natural mode of locomotion; therefore, Sagittarians love to walk, run, and travel the world over. In addition, it governs the sciatic nerve, the longest nerve in the body. Those with a strong Sagittarian influence in their horoscopes often develop problems with this nerve, which is sometimes related to a lack of the mineral silica associated with this sign.

♑ CAPRICORN

Capricorn ushers in the Winter Solstice when darkness begins to give way to light as the days gradually become longer. This increase in light has been celebrated in all ancient civilizations, culminating in the birth of Christ and the subsequent celebration of Christmas.

Capricorn is symbolized by the mountain goat who gradually and surefootedly ascends the mountain. Patience and perseverance enable Capricorns to reach the top, despite many obstacles. Capricorn has the body of a fish and the upper torso and head of a goat; the goat's horns symbolize the lunar crescents. The fish represents the Moon goddess as ruler of the waters. In Babylonia and Sumeria, the Moon as goddess of the sea was depicted in mermaid form as a fish or dolphin. (In Asian zodiacs, the same sign is portrayed as a dolphin.) The goat is related to the goddess of healing. The goddess of healing worshipped in Libya and Thrace was Aegis, meaning "protection" and "guidance." She was represented by a goat because the goat is sure-footed and also a milk-producing animal. The priestesses of Aegis specialized in medicine and wore aprons made of goatskins. This goddess was also named Hygeia or "health" because of the cures she brought about.

Capricorn rules the knees. In order for Capricorns to reach their goals, they must learn to "bend the knee," or acknowledge something higher than themselves. The evolved Capricornian is personified in the spiritual seeker who is able to ascend the heights. Capricorn is also the sign of the business executive, teacher, and manager. Capricorns can tend to be cold, distant, and crystallized in their ideas and often patronizing to those they consider beneath them. They can also portray the more positive aspects of Saturn, Capricorn's ruling planet, by personifying the teacher of wisdom who incorporates discipline and responsibility in manifesting ultimate faith.

In addition to the knees, Capricorn rules the structural elements in the body—the spine, teeth, bones, joints, ligaments, and skin. When Capricorns become too set in their thinking, crystallization may develop in the body, manifesting symptoms such as arthritis and rheumatism.

♒ AQUARIUS

Aquarius opens up new dimensions in its focus on vibrations and electrical force fields. Although Aquarius is an air sign, it is depicted as a Water Bearer, a human carrying an urn of water and offering it to all of humanity. The original symbol of Aquarius was a woman bearing a water jug (as in the Star card of the Tarot in the Rider deck). In Egyptian hieroglyphics, the sacred water jar was the symbol of the goddess Nut and of femininity, the vessel representing the female genital organs.

Aquarius is the humanitarian, giving forth the water of life to all whom it will nurture. Ruled by the planet Uranus, Aquarians are the first to bring forth new ideas and inventions and are always ahead of their peers, being innovative and often eccentric. When Aquarians become too mental and too involved in the realm of ideas, they tend to be cold and distant. (Aquarius is the sign furthest away from Leo, the sign ruled by the Sun.) Aquarians want to make their ideas available to all, regardless of their social or financial status. In doing so, they may react to the Capricornian conservatism by becoming too rebellious, eccentric, or perverse. They may also be too idealistic and need to ground their visions in a deeper reality.

Physiologically, Aquarius rules the circulatory system and the ankles. If one is not connected to the heart energy (the love and warmth symbolized by Leo and the Sun), one may tend to have poor circulation and cold extremities.

♓ PISCES

The sign Pisces is symbolized by the two fishes, one swimming upstream and one moving downstream. The unevolved Piscean might have some inner conflicts that result in indecisiveness and being "wishy-washy"; in the more evolved type, the fishes are in balance, as in the yin/yang symbol. The fish represents Christ. The Greek initials I.C.H.T.H.U.S. (standing for Jesus Christ, Son of God, Savior) made an acronym that spelled "fish." The symbol was adapted because the Vernal Equinox was moving into the sign of the fishes, ushering in the Piscean age. Many of Jesus' disciples were fishermen who renounced the world and followed him. Evolved Pisceans often renounce material goods in order to attain spiritual enlightenment.

The two fishes also represent the real and imaginary worlds. Imagination may devolve into illusion or escapism, as in the use of addictive substances. Positively, it may manifest in the arts—music, photography, or theatrical achievements. Since Pisces rules the feet, Pisceans also exhibit their creative energy in the dance world. Ruled by the planet Neptune, Pisceans are often involved in the fields of healing, dreamwork, and metaphysical activities.

Physiologically, Pisces rules the lymphatic system. When these natives hold back their emotions, the lymphatic system can become congested, giving rise to swollen lymph glands and nodes.

The Twelve Houses

The house divisions in the horoscope are based on the Earth's rotation on its axis. The Earth turns on its axis every 24 hours, causing the cycles of day and night. Because of the Sun's path through the ecliptic, a different sign rises at dawn at different times of the year. The time of day determines which sign will be rising and what the Ascendant of the individual horoscope will be. The house cusps start with the Ascendant or rising degree.

In Holistic Astrology, the houses are considered in relationship to the time of day they represent. Therefore, we move clockwise instead of counterclockwise and begin with the twelfth house.

As the Ascendant is dawn, the **twelfth house** is from 6–8 A.M. The day's energies are beginning at this time, and planets in the twelfth house may represent strong qualities the individual has that are not always visible to others since this is still a dark time or seed time. These planets may also represent traits or experiences the individual has in early years when first beginning life on the planet. As these traits are cultivated, they become stronger. (Perhaps this is why so much astrological research has shown the strength of twelfth house planets in determining what an individual does.)

The **eleventh house** covers 8–10 A.M., the time that one begins to move outside and make contact with others in whatever projects one is involved with. In traditional astrology, this house rules friendships and group relationships.

The **tenth** or **Midheaven house** equates to the Sun's zenith, high noon (10 A.M.–12 P.M.). Planets in this house show the energies that will manifest the strongest out in the world and will be obvious to everyone that encounters the individual. We think of this house as profession and social standing, as well as an indication of leadership abilities. Many well-known people have several tenth house planets.

The **ninth house** corresponds to 12–2 P.M., often regarded as a quiet time or siesta time after the noon meal. This is a time when one rests and goes within oneself; it is an expansive time in an inner sense, giving this house correspondence to philosophical ideas, metaphysics, and journeys to places that expand our awareness and provide us with new insights.

From 2–4 P.M. we are back in the world, but in a different way. We have had our afternoon rest and can now relate to things in a fresh or new manner. Perhaps this resembles the quality of transformation that the **eighth house** represents. There is a transcendence here of ordinary reality, a letting go and a moving beyond.

From 4–6 P.M. it is a time for completion, for ending a cycle, and for planning the evening meal and activities. In keeping with the **seventh house**, we may spend more time with those close to us as we return to our homes and prepare to go inside ourselves for the dark hours.

With the **sixth house** we have moved below the horizon into the inner worlds and away from the light of the Sun. During this time period (6–8 P.M.), we may refresh our energies through some type of meditation, food, and relaxation. It is a time when we serve ourselves and our physical bodies.

The **fifth house** (8–10 P.M.) is generally a time of play and relaxation. Evening activities often include sports, entertainment, and enjoying group or family activities.

The **fourth house** (10 P.M.–12 A.M.) represents a very deep time where we move into another state of consciousness through sleep. Here we encounter the very core of our being and get in touch with our most unconscious thoughts and processes. This house is at the bottom of the wheel, where we are rooted and grounded to the Earth, yet exist deeply within our own sphere.

The **third house** (12–2 A.M.) is a time period when we access so many of our unconscious thought processes and motivations. If the third house represents our mind and autonomic nervous system, we can understand how this is related to the hours when we exist in this other state.

The **second house** (2–4 A.M.) is perhaps a time when many ideas and creative projects are seeded while we remain in the state of sleep. It is a time before dawn when our connections to the Earth begin to surface. The second house is often considered a house of attachments to material things or to ideas.

And now we come to the **first house**, the glorious moments of dawn when we see the first light and begin to experience our beings back in the physical state again. This is truly a beginning of our relationship to the Earth, our adapting whatever forms we can to accomplish our mission here. Thus, the first house relates to our physical vehicles, to our "personas," to the tentative way we begin our Earth walk.

Planetary Rulership over Vitamins and Minerals

Just as the planets and signs govern various physiological processes in our bodies, so do they rule the vitamins and minerals necessary for our growth and balance. We can obtain these nutrients from foods, herbs, dietary supplements, and from working with vibratory forms of healing such as color therapy, music therapy, crystals, and gems. These modalities help to transform certain imbalances within our physical, emotional, and spiritual bodies.

How then do we determine which vitamins and minerals we need by using our horoscope? First, we must analyze the chart as outlined in the introductory chapter. The **lack** of certain elements in the horoscope may indicate the need for particular nutrients; for example, one who lacks fire looks under the fire planets and finds that the Sun rules vitamin D, Mars rules iron, and Jupiter rules silica and chromium. Iron is often required by one lacking fire; vitamin D, silica, and chromium may be necessary, but it is important to use one of the confirming tools to check out the individual and the lack of these substances. In the case of **excess** elements, excess air would tend to make one very nervous and anxious. Referring to the correspondences to the air planets Mercury and Uranus, we find the B complex vitamins, magnesium, and manganese—all of these support the nervous system.

There is no one way to work with these nutrients; it may be that a lack of an element suggests vitamins or minerals ruled by a corresponding planet, or it may be that an excess of the element does. Again, this needs to be confirmed in the person's body.

One next examines the **Sun, Moon, Ascendant** and their aspects. Hard aspects to the Sun, Moon, or Ascendant in Sagittarius may indicate a lack of silica or chromium ruled by Jupiter, especially when combined with hard aspects to Saturn or Neptune. A Taurus Sun, Moon, or Ascendant receiving hard aspects may indicate potential thyroid difficulty, resulting in a lack of iodine or copper ruled by Venus.

Examining the **sixth house** for planets and the ruler, we may find Neptune in the house or Pisces on the cusp. This indicates conditions that are difficult to diagnose; it also may indicate a weak immune system necessitating more vitamins C and A as well as zinc and potassium ruled by Neptune. This information needs to be confirmed by the body.

After studying the natal horoscope, consider the **transits** and **progressions** to the planets, Ascendant, and Midheaven. With transits and progressions, the hard aspects as well as the inconjuncts should be noted. Under transits of Saturn, one tends to have problems with the teeth and bones and needs more calcium; Uranus transits call for more B complex, magnesium, and manganese to nourish the nervous system (and a lot more exercise!). Neptune transits often bring on allergies and lowered immune system response; plenty of vitamins A, C, bioflavonoids, zinc, and potassium are usually required. Transits of Pluto may affect the hormonal balance, the reproductive system, and the excretory system; often vitamin E and selenium are needed.

SUN

Vitamin D

The Sun rules vitamin D, the sunshine vitamin. Ultraviolet rays from the Sun activate cholesterol-related substances in the skin, which are then transformed to vitamin D, which in turn acts with a parathyroid hormone to regulate calcium metabolism. Vitamin D facilitates the absorption of calcium from the intestinal tract and aids in the assimilation of phosphorus, which is required for bone formation. If there is not enough calcium in the intestinal tract, the body absorbs it from the bones themselves.

Since vitamin D is a fat-soluble vitamin, it does not dissolve in water and therefore is not easily excreted in the urine. If taken in large quantities, it tends to accumulate, and there may be difficulty getting rid of the excess. When too much vitamin D is taken, so much calcium can be absorbed and removed from the bones that it begins to form deposits that damage the tissues of the heart, blood vessels, and lungs.

For those individuals who live in northern climates, vitamin D can be obtained naturally through diet since it is found in large amounts in fish liver oil. (Fish eat plankton, which thrive near the surface of the sea and are exposed to sunlight. However, much fish liver oil today is toxic.) Other good sources of vitamin D besides fish liver are organic calves' liver, chicken liver, beef liver, fertile egg yolks, yogurt, and soured milk products. (The myth of milk being a source of vitamin D should be clarified. The vitamin added to milk is a form of vitamin D—D-2, or ergocalciferol. This synthetic form is made by taking a substance produced by yeast called *ergosterol* and exposing it to ultraviolet radiation. The ergosterol is then separated, purified, and added to milk.) For vegetarians, vitamin D can be obtained from the Sun, and sufficient calcium from leafy green vegetables.

MOON
No vitamins or minerals are ruled by the Moon.

MERCURY

B Complex
Since Mercury rules the nervous system, it is related to the B complex vitamins, water soluble substances that can be cultivated from bacteria, yeasts, fungi, or molds. Known B complex vitamins include B-1 (thiamine), B-2 (riboflavin), B-3 (niacin), B-6 (pyridoxine), B-12 (cyanocobalamin), B-13 (orotic acid), B-15 (pangamic acid), biotin, choline, folic acid, inositol, PABA (para-aminobenzoic acid), and B-17 (laetrile or amygdalin). All of these vitamins are grouped together because they are found in the same foods, have a close relationship in vegetable and animal tissues, and work together in maintaining certain body functions.

The B vitamins are necessary for the normal functioning of the nervous system. They provide the body with energy by converting carbohydrates into glucose, which is then burned by the body. They also are important in maintaining muscle tone in the gastrointestinal tract. Since B vitamins are not stored in the body, their excess amounts are secreted, and they need to be continually replaced. Sugar and alcohol destroy B vitamins; certain drugs, insecticides, and estrogen create a condition in the intestinal tract that can destroy the B vitamins.

Deficiencies of the B complex result in malfunctions of the nervous system like insomnia, irritability, nervousness, depression, dizziness, and headaches. Severe deficiencies may manifest as anemia, baldness, grey hair, acne and skin problems, constipation, and high cholesterol level.

The richest sources of the B complex are whole grains such as buckwheat, millet, brown rice, oats, rye, quinoa, and amaranth. Liver is especially rich in B-12; however, only organic liver should be eaten because of the liver's tendency to concentrate contaminants. Nutritional yeast, a strong source of the B complex, has been recommended by many nutritional experts, but many individuals tend to be allergic to yeast. For those who are not, it still has a strongly acidic effect on the body. (It has been shown that uric acid levels were elevated after using three tablespoons of yeast a day.)

VENUS

Venus rules the thyroid and thus is related to the mineral iodine. It also rules copper, sodium and the bioflavonoids, or vitamin P. The sodium/potassium balance, or acid/alkaline balance, is a function of the kidneys, ruled by the sign Libra and the planet Venus. (Neptune is a higher octave of Venus and rules potassium.) The bioflavonoids, particularly rutin (found in buckwheat), are important nutrients for the kidneys.

Iodine

Iodine is one of the most important trace minerals since it is an integral part of thyroxine, the principal hormone produced by the thyroid gland. Iodine helps regulate energy production, promotes growth and development, and stimulates the rate of metabolism, helping the body to burn excess fat. When thyroxine production is normal, the synthesis of cholesterol is stimulated, carotene is converted to vitamin A, and the absorption of carbohydrates from the intestine works more efficiently. Care should be taken in using iodine supplements as large doses of iodine may impair the synthesis of thyroid hormones.

An iodine deficiency can result in goiter, characterized by thyroid enlargement or hypothyroidism. It can eventually lead to hardening of the arteries, obesity, sluggish metabolism, slow mental reactions, rapid pulse, and heart palpitation.

Iodine is found in all sea vegetables, particularly dulse, and in ocean fish and seafood.

Copper

Just as Venus and Mars work together in combining their energies, copper (ruled by Venus) assists in the formation of hemoglobin and red blood cells by facilitating iron (ruled by Mars) absorption. Copper is required for the synthesis of phospholipids and helps the body to oxidize vitamin C, working with it to form elastin.

Copper and zinc have an inverse relation to each other. (Zinc is ruled by Neptune.) When copper levels are high, zinc levels are low. Too much copper tends to produce epileptic-type seizures. Too little copper may predispose one to cardiovascular disease.

Foods high in copper include organic liver, sea vegetables, fish, and green leafy vegetables.

Sodium

Sodium, along with potassium, equalizes the acid/ alkaline factor in the blood and helps regulate water balance within the body. Sodium and potassium are also involved in muscle contraction and expansion and in nerve stimulation. Sodium is absorbed in the small intestine and stomach and then filtered out and carried by the blood to the kidneys. The excess is excreted in the urine. The adrenal hormone aldosterone regulates sodium metabolism.

Excesses of sodium, found much more commonly than deficiencies, may cause abnormal fluid retention accompanied by dizziness and swelling of ankles, legs, and face. Excess sodium also contributes to high blood pressure. To balance an excess sodium condition, eliminate salt, red meats, soy sauce, and miso soup (which tends to be high in sodium). Other foods high in sodium include sea vegetables as dulse, hijiki, arame, nori, wakame, kombu, kelp, seafoods, all meat, and poultry.

Bioflavonoids

Bioflavonoids, or vitamin P, are composed of a group of substances that appear in fruits and vegetables in conjunction with vitamin C. The components of bioflavonoids are citrin, hesperidin, rutin, flavones, and flavonals.

Bioflavonoids were discovered in the white segments of citrus fruits. They are important in the absorption and use of vitamin C. They help vitamin C by keeping collagen, the intracellular cement, in healthy condition. They increase the strength of the capillaries, help prevent hemorrhage in the capillaries and connective tissues, and build a protective barrier against infections.

Bioflavonoids are also important in alleviating allergies and asthma. Along with vitamin C, they are helpful in treating bleeding gums, eczema, rheumatism, and rheumatic fever. Vitamin P is also beneficial in the treatment of muscular dystrophy because it helps lower blood pressure. Rutin is a major remedy for ailments of the kidneys.

Deficiency symptoms are related to vitamin C deficiencies and include the increased tendency to hemorrhage and bruise easily.

Vitamin P is found in buckwheat, buckwheat sprouts, rose hips, lemons, blackberries, black currants, grapes, cherries, grapefruits, and oranges.

MARS

Iron

Mars rules iron, the major function of which is to combine with protein and copper in making hemoglobin. Hemoglobin transports oxygen in the blood from the lungs to the tissues. Iron is also necessary for the formation of myoglobin found in the muscle tissue. Myoglobin supplies oxygen to the muscle cells in order to enable the muscles to contract.

Iron is a difficult mineral to absorb; it is absorbed in the upper part of the small intestine and stored in the liver, spleen, bone marrow, and blood. Very little iron is excreted in the urine. Vitamin E aids in iron assimilation, but too much vitamin E taken at the same time can hinder this process. Excess phosphorus hinders iron absorption. In addition, the lack of hydrochloric acid and a high intake of coffee and tea all interfere with iron integration. Protein promotes iron absorption since certain amino acids tend to chelate the iron and help carry it into the system. The absorption of chelated forms of iron is greater than that of the free ionic form.

The most common deficiency of iron is iron deficient anemia, in which the amount of hemoglobin in the red blood cells is reduced and the cells become smaller. Symptoms of anemia are fatigue, pale skin, difficulty breathing, and decreased resistance to disease.

Foods high in iron include organic liver, wheatgrass juice, sea vegetables (especially dulse), blackstrap molasses, beets, red cabbage, fish, red chard, cherries, black mission figs, and prunes. The herbs nettle leaf, yellow dock root, and burdock root are especially high in iron and can all be made into teas.

JUPITER

Silica

Jupiter rules the trace minerals silica and chromium. The cell salt silica is associated with the sign Sagittarius. Silica is an important trace mineral since it is involved with calcium assimilation. It provides for strong bones and nails and gives the glossy shine to the hair as well. It helps to keep the pores of the skin open and the enamel of the teeth strong. Silica is also involved with vision.

Deficiencies of silica include abscesses, boils, and other skin conditions; sties and ulcers of the cornea; hair that falls out; white spots on the nails; and swollen parotid glands.

Foods high in silica include sea vegetables, like wakame, kombu, kelp, and arame, and green leafy vegetables. The herb horsetail grass is an excellent source of silica.

Chromium

Since Jupiter rules the pancreas, which regulates metabolism, it is involved with the trace mineral chromium. Chromium is essential in producing an enzyme-like substance called GTF, or Glucose Tolerance Factor, a substance necessary in the production and utilization of insulin.

When chromium is deficient, elevated blood sugar levels or diabetes may exist. Arteriosclerosis and plaque in the arteries are also related to chromium deficiency.

It is difficult to find many food sources for chromium; it is found primarily in yeast, which is a very acidic food. However, whole grains also contain chromium.

SATURN

Saturn is related to the minerals calcium and phosphorus, which are required for bones, joints, teeth, and skeletal development. It also rules sulfur, which is found in keratin, a protein substance necessary for the skin, hair, and nails.

Calcium

Calcium is the most abundant mineral in the body, with 99% deposited in the bones and teeth. The remaining 1% is in the soft tissue. Calcium's major role, in combination with phosphorus, is to build and maintain bones and teeth. Calcium is also essential for the contraction of muscles. If the muscle doesn't have enough calcium, the fibers are motionless and do not slide together and mesh. Therefore, the muscle cannot contract, or once it has contracted it will not relax, causing a "cramp." Along with magnesium, calcium is important in maintaining a healthy nervous system. It assists in the process of blood clotting and helps prevent the accumulation of too much acid or alkali in the blood. It also aids in the body's utilization of iron, helps activate several enzymes, and regulates the passage of nutrients in and out of the cell walls.

Calcium absorption is inefficient; usually only 20%–30% of ingested calcium is absorbed. Calcium integration depends on the presence of adequate amounts of vitamin D, which works with the parathyroid hormone to regulate the amount of calcium in the blood. Certain substances interfere with calcium absorption. When excessive amounts of fat combine with calcium, an insoluble compound is formed that cannot be absorbed. Oxalic acid, found in chocolate, spinach, and rhubarb, makes an insoluble compound and may form into kidney or gallbladder stones. Large amounts of phytic acid, present in the bran of grains, may also tie up calcium absorption. Protein is also important. Too little protein will result in reduced absorption, while a high intake of animal protein can depress calcium retention. When a person is inactive, calcium tends to be extracted from the bones to be used for other purposes. This is especially true of older people who exercise less. After the hormonal shifts of menopause, women seem to be more susceptible to the action of the parathyroid hormone, which promotes the removal of calcium from the bones. The result is a gradual demineralizing of the bones with age and a tendency toward osteoporosis and increased fractures.

Calcium is found in turnip and carrot juice, green leafy vegetables such as kale, mustard greens, collard greens, chard, bok choy, and dandelion greens, sea vegetables, and soured milk products. The herbs comfrey root and leaf, wintergreen, oatstraw, sarsaparilla root, alfalfa, borage, and plantain contain significant amounts of calcium.

Phosphorus

Phosphorus is the second most abundant mineral in the body. Phosphorus plays a part in almost every chemical reaction in the body since it is present in every cell. It helps in the utilization of carbohydrates, fats, and protein for the repair of cells and the production of energy. It stimulates muscle contractions, including the contraction of the heart muscle. Phosphorus is an essential part of nucleoproteins, which are responsible for cell division and reproduction and transference of hereditary traits. It is also necessary for proper skeletal growth, tooth development, and kidney functioning. Phosphorus speeds up the healing process in bone fractures and reduces the loss of calcium; it has been used successfully in the treatment of osteomalacia and osteoporosis. It is helpful in treating arthritic conditions and disorders of the teeth and gums.

An insufficient amount of phosphorus may result in stunted growth, poor quality of bones and teeth, and other bone disorders. A deficiency in the calcium/phosphorus balance can cause arthritis, pyorrhea, rickets, or tooth decay. Phosphorus absorption depends on the presence of vitamin D and calcium.

Phosphorus is found in whole grains, seeds, nuts, eggs, fish, organic poultry, and organic meat.

Sulfur

Sulfur has an important relationship with protein, as it is contained in the amino acids methionine, cystine, and cysteine, and is necessary for collagen synthesis. It is found in keratin, the protein substance necessary for the maintenance of skin, hair, and nails. Sulfur is important in tissue respiration where oxygen and other substances are used to build cells and release energy.

Sulfur is helpful in treating arthritis; the level of cystine, a sulfur-containing amino acid, is lower than normal in arthritic patients. It is also used topically in the form of an ointment in treating skin disorders.

Certain vegetables like cabbage, broccoli, brussels sprouts, cauliflower, eggs, fish, and organic meats contain large amounts of sulfur.

URANUS

Since Uranus rules the nervous system and electrical conduction system in the body, the minerals magnesium and manganese are related to Uranus, and are very important in balancing the nervous system.

Magnesium

Nearly 70% of the body's magnesium is located in the bones along with calcium and phosphorus, while 30% is found in the soft tissues and body fluids. Magnesium is important in activating the enzymes necessary for the metabolism of carbohydrates and amino acids. It balances the effect of calcium, thereby playing a significant role in neuromuscular contractions. It helps regulate the acid/alkaline balance in the body and promotes absorption of other minerals like calcium, phosphorus, sodium, and potassium. Magnesium enables one to utilize the B complex, C, and E vitamins. It is important for the proper functioning of the nerves and muscles, especially the heart muscle. The need for magnesium is increased when blood cholesterol levels are high and when consumption of protein is high.

Magnesium is important in maintaining the electrical energy system in the body. It is vital in preventing heart attacks and coronary thrombosis. It has also proved beneficial in the treatment of neuromuscular disorders, nervousness, tantrums, and hand tremors. Magnesium, rather than calcium, forms the kind of hard tooth enamel that resists decay. No matter how much calcium is ingested, only a soft enamel will be found unless magnesium is present. Magnesium also helps protect from an accumulation of calcium deposits in the urinary tract by making the calcium and phosphorus soluble in the urine, preventing them from turning into stones. It has been used in controlling convulsions in epileptic patients. Since magnesium is very alkaline, it has been used as an antacid in place of antacid compounds.

Symptoms of magnesium deficiency include anxiety, confusion, muscle twitches, tremors, cramps, and spasms. An inadequate supply of magnesium may result in the formation of clots in the heart and brain and may contribute to calcium deposits in the kidneys, blood vessels, and heart. One of the first steps in treating magnesium deficiencies, among children especially, is to eliminate milk from the diet. Milk contains high amounts of calciferol, a synthetic vitamin D that binds with magnesium and carries it out of the body.

Magnesium is found in high amounts in green leafy vegetables since it is an essential component of chlorophyll. (It has the same relationship to chlorophyll that iron has to hemoglobin; that is, it transports nutrients through a plant's vascular system.) It is also found in oil-rich seeds and nuts, especially filberts, almonds, and cashews. The herbs alfalfa, borage, and red raspberry leaf contain significant amounts of magnesium.

Manganese

Manganese, a trace mineral that is extremely important in nourishing the brain and nervous system, also supports the connective tissue that provides the framework for the bones. In experimental animals, manganese deficiencies produced bone deformities that were not due to a lack of calcium but to a failure of the bone to stretch out to its normal length and shape.

Manganese is beneficial in the treatment of diabetes; diabetics who were unresponsive to insulin were able to control their symptoms by drinking alfalfa tea, which contains large amounts of manganese. Patients with allergies, schizophrenia, Parkinson's disease and myasthenia gravis (failure of muscular coordination and loss of muscle strength) respond well to manganese supplementation. In schizophrenic and allergic patients, manganese helps to restore balance when histamine, the substance that is released during allergic and schizoid reactions, is either too high or too low in the blood.

A deficiency of manganese can affect glucose tolerance, resulting in the inability to remove excess sugar from the blood by oxidation or storage. Ataxia, the failure of muscular coordination, has been linked with an inadequate intake of manganese. Deficiencies may also lead to paralysis and concussions in infants, and dizziness, ear noises, and loss of hearing in adults.

Manganese is found in blueberries, boysenberries, and other dark blue berries like olallie berries. It is also contained in alfalfa sprouts, whole grains, and leafy green vegetables. The herb alfalfa is high in manganese.

NEPTUNE

Neptune is related to vitamin C and zinc, both of which play an important role in nourishing the immune system, which Neptune rules. Neptune also rules vitamin A since it is connected with the eyes and inner sight. In addition, Neptune rules potassium, which is related to the acid/alkaline balance; this balance is often unstable in strong Neptunian individuals, who require a great deal of potassium.

Vitamin C

Vitamin C has had such dramatic effects on various body conditions and disease states that too much of it tends to be used, especially in its acidic forms, thus creating an acid/alkaline imbalance in the body. Vitamin C should be used as Ester-C, preferably with magnesium. Vitamin C should also be used in conjunction with the bioflavonoids or vitamin P, alternating between vitamin

C one day and bioflavonoids the following day, since they help the vitamin C to assimilate in the body.

One of the primary functions of vitamin C is maintaining collagen, a protein necessary for the formation of connective tissue in skin, ligaments, and bones, which is why it is used for healing wounds and burns. It also fights bacterial infections and reduces the effects on the body of certain allergy-producing substances. It helps in forming red blood cells and preventing hemorrhaging.

When cultures of human cells were bathed in a solution containing vitamin C, they were able to produce large quantities of a substance known as *interferon*, which "interferes" with the ability of viruses to invade cells. There is also some evidence that vitamin C exerts a detoxifying effect in those who have been exposed to heavy metals like lead and cadmium. High doses seem to have a protective effect against pesticides and food additives.

One should be careful in taking large doses of vitamin C, however, as it can interfere with calcium absorption. Vitamin C is sometimes converted to calcium oxalate in the urine, which can result in the formation of kidney stones.

A deficiency of vitamin C results in swollen or painful joints, a tendency to bruise easily, bleeding gums, pyorrhea, tooth decay, nosebleeds, lowered resistance to infections, and slow healing of wounds and fractures. A severe deficiency results in scurvy. Smoking tobacco lowers the blood level of vitamin C.

Ascorbic acid is found in most fruits and vegetables—especially leafy green and yellow vegetables, green peppers, citrus fruits, rose hips, acerola berries, and tomatoes. However, it is recommended that green and yellow vegetables be used as primary sources since so many people are allergic to citrus and tomatoes, both of which are extremely acidic. (Despite what the nutrition books say about citrus becoming alkaline in the body, eating a lot of citrus fruit often leads to canker sores and other sores around the mouth. One of the reasons why so many people are allergic to citrus is that it is picked from the tree before it is ripe.) Sprouts made from the seeds of grains and beans, such as alfalfa, red clover, sunflower, buckwheat, lentil, and mung bean, are exceptionally high in vitamin C.

Zinc

Zinc is found in the body in larger amounts than any other trace mineral except for iron. Zinc is essential for the growth and development of the reproductive organs and for normal functioning of the prostate gland. Zinc is found in high concentrations in the prostate gland and the semen, and zinc supplements have been used to treat prostate problems and retarded development of the genital organs.

Zinc is important in healing wounds and burns since it is involved in certain enzymes that produce new cells and form keratin, a substance present in hair, nails, and skin. Zinc is also an effective treatment for acne. Since it helps eliminate cholesterol deposits, it has been used successfully in the treatment of atherosclerosis. It has also been used in treating cirrhosis of the liver and alcoholism. Because it regulates the effect of insulin in the blood, it is beneficial for diabetics.

Signs of zinc deficiency are stretch marks on the skin and white spots on the fingernails. Other symptoms are abnormal fatigue, poor appetite, a loss of taste sensitivity, and retarded growth. Zinc deficiency makes one more susceptible to infection and prolongs the healing of wounds. Recent studies show that sustained zinc deficiency causes sterility and dwarfism in humans and leads to changes in the size and structure of the prostate gland.

Foods high in zinc include oysters, pumpkin seeds, sea vegetables, and fish.

Vitamin A

Vitamin A is essential in the formation of visual purple, a substance in the eye that is necessary for proper night vision. It is also important in treating infections and in resistance to infection. Many infections that respond dramatically to vitamin A occur in the protective covering of the body, the mucous membranes that line the respiratory passages, the gastrointestinal tract, the urinary passages, and the eyes, ears, and nose.

Vitamin A is found in two forms: preformed vitamin A, or retinol, which is present in large amounts in animal and fish livers, and beta-carotene, one of the carotene pigments found in green and yellow vegetables and fruits. Green leafy vegetables are even richer in usable carotene than carrots.

Vitamin A toxicity can occur if too much of this vitamin is ingested. This often occurs as a result of preformed A taken in fish liver oil capsules; very little toxicity has occurred from beta-carotene. Symptoms of vitamin A toxicity include nausea, vomiting, diarrhea, dry skin, hair loss, headaches, sore lips, and flaky, itchy skin.

Factors interfering with vitamin A absorption include excessive consumption of alcohol, too much iron, the use of cortisone and other drugs, gastrointestinal and liver disorders, and any obstructions of the bile duct.

Deficiencies of vitamin A include night blindness, an inability of the eyes to adjust to darkness, other eye diseases, and rough, dry, or prematurely aged skin. Severe conditions include corneal ulcers and softening of the bones and teeth since a deficiency of vitamin A leads to the loss of vitamin C.

The richest source of vitamin A is hot red peppers; other sources are green leafy vegetables and orange vegetables and fruits like carrots, sweet potatoes, winter squashes, and apricots. Although vitamin A is found in high amounts in fish liver, this would not be a recommended source at this time due to the high level of toxic residues in the livers and other organs of fish.

Potassium

Potassium and sodium are alkalis; they have a single electrical charge instead of the two charges of most other minerals. Therefore, they tend to move readily through solutions, especially water. Potassium tends to be concentrated inside the cell, whereas sodium is more abundant in the fluid surrounding the cell. Sodium is found in the waters on the Earth's surface while potassium is concentrated inside the plants. Potassium and sodium help regulate water balance within the body. Potassium is necessary to preserve the proper alkalinity of the body fluids. It assists the conversion of glucose and glycogen (the form in which glucose is stored in the liver). It stimulates the kidneys to eliminate body toxins and wastes. Potassium is also important in maintaining the skin in good health. With sodium, it normalizes the heartbeat and nourishes the muscular system. It also unites with phosphorus to send oxygen to the brain and works with calcium in the regulation of neuromuscular activity.

Potassium is absorbed from the small intestine. It is excreted through urination and perspiration. Aldosterone, an adrenal hormone, stimulates potassium excretion. Excessive use of salt depletes the body's conservation of potassium. Potassium can also be depleted by prolonged diarrhea, vomiting, and excessive sweating. Contrary to the theory of losing sodium through excessive sweating and replacing it with salt tablets, it is actually potassium that is lost. Both alcohol and coffee increase the excretion of potassium; excessive intake of sugar also increases potassium excretions. Low blood sugar levels strain the adrenal glands causing additional potassium to be lost in the urine, while causing water and salt to be held in the tissues. An adequate supply of magnesium is needed to retain the storage of potassium in the cells.

Potassium has been used to treat cases of high blood pressure caused by excess sodium intake. Potassium chloride is also effective in treating allergies. Giving potassium to diabetic patients has reduced blood pressure and blood sugar levels.

Symptoms of potassium deficiency may include nervous disorders, insomnia, constipation, slow and irregular heartbeat and muscle damage, acne and dry skin conditions. When a deficiency of potassium impairs glucose metabolism, energy is no longer available to the muscles and they may become paralyzed. Infants who have diarrhea may have a potassium deficiency because the passage of the intestinal contents is so rapid as to decrease its absorption. Diabetic patients are often deficient in potassium, as are those who take hormone drugs like cortisone and aldosterone, which cause sodium to be retained.

Food sources high in potassium include potatoes, leafy green vegetables, and bananas; the herbs plantain and alfalfa are also high in potassium.

PLUTO

Pluto rules the reproductive and excretory systems and thus is related to vitamin E and the trace mineral selenium, both of which help to balance the hormonal system.

Vitamin E

Vitamin E is a fat-soluble vitamin composed of a group of compounds called *tocopherols*. (*Tocopherol* means "bringing forth normal births.") Alpha tocopherol is the most potent form of vitamin E and has the greatest nutritional and biological value. Tocopherols occur in the highest concentrations in cold-pressed vegetable oils, raw seeds and nuts, and soybeans. Vitamin E was first obtained from wheat germ.

Vitamin E is an antioxidant, meaning that it opposes oxidation of vital substances in the body. It prevents saturated fatty acids and vitamin A from breaking down and combining with other substances. Fats and oils containing vitamin E are less susceptible to rancidity than those devoid of it.

In areas where there is high air pollution, vitamin E has proved helpful. Air polluted with combinations of ozone and oxides of metals like nitrogen, cadmium, and lead makes us need increasing amounts of protective antioxidants like vitamin E. These oxidating reactions (peroxidation) also enter the body through food. The principal sources of reactive oxygenation in food are vegetable oils that have become rancid. When peroxidation occurs, it produces a pigment that causes discoloration in the tissues. These deposits show up in the fatty tissue and the skin of those who are advanced in age. Rats exposed to high concentrations of oxygen were fed large amounts of wheat germ oil, and they lived their normal life span.

Vitamin E also plays an important role in preventing heart disease since it makes it possible for the cardiac muscle to function with less oxygen, thereby increasing endurance and stamina. It causes dilation of the blood vessels, permitting a fuller flow of blood to the heart. Vitamin E is also helpful in the functioning of the reproductive organs. Rats on a diet in which vitamin E was absent failed to reproduce. It has been used to regulate flow during menstruation and as a treatment for "hot flashes" and headaches during menopause. Applied as an ointment, vitamin E aids in healing burns and skin ulcers and dissolves scar tissue.

A vitamin E deficiency is not responsible for any deficiency diseases, but its lack may lead to many other conditions. The first sign of vitamin E depletion is the rupture of red blood cells, which results from their increased fragility. A deficiency may result in abnormal fat deposits in the muscles and an increased demand for oxygen. Iron absorption and hemoglobin formation are also impaired. The amount of vitamin E consumed should be carefully regulated, especially in those with high blood pressure or rheumatic heart disease. If iron supplements are being taken, they should be used at a different time of the day, as iron metabolism is impaired by too much vitamin E.

Food sources rich in vitamin E include vegetable oils, seeds, nuts, and soybeans.

Selenium

Selenium is a trace mineral that works closely with vitamin E in its metabolic actions and in the promotion of normal body growth and fertility. Selenium supplements have been helpful to women during menopause and at other times when they were undergoing hormonal changes. As a natural antioxidant, selenium helps preserve the elasticity of tissues by delaying the oxidation of polyunsaturated fatty acids. Demonstrations with mice showed that selenium increased resistance to disease by increasing the number of antibodies that neutralize toxins.

Rich natural sources of selenium are green leafy vegetables such as kale, Swiss chard, mustard greens, turnip greens, dandelion greens, and chicory, also cabbage, broccoli, and asparagus. Rice polishings and the bran and germ of whole grains also contain selenium.

Herbs and
Astrological Signs

Herbology is a complex study; it is not always easy to determine which herbs to utilize simply by studying the astrological horoscope. Complete knowledge of the patient's symptoms and health history needs to be considered. Make a thorough study of the client's horoscope as outlined in the introductory chapter. Other diagnostic tools like pulse diagnosis, iridology, or radiesthesia (the use of the pendulum) should also be employed before recommending any herbal remedies.

Paracelsus, the father of modern medicine, said that for every star in the sky there is a flower in the meadow, and that all growing things reveal their usefulness through their structure, form, color, and aroma. He advised healers to search within themselves for the insights by which they could sense the energies of plants. He also stated that the blossoms follow the motions of the planets, some opening their petals according to phases of the Moon, others by the cycle of the Sun, and others as a response to various stars.

Nicholas Culpeper in his *Complete Herbal* (W. Foulsham and Co.), Chapter 15, gives the following rules for utilizing herbal medicines in conjunction with the horoscope:

> 1. "Fortify the body with herbs of the nature of the Lord of the Ascendant; 'tis no matter whether he be a Fortune or Infortune in

this case." [Strengthen your body with herbs belonging to the planet ruling the rising sign. Thus, if Capricorn is rising, one should use the herbs of Saturn.]

2. "Let your medicine be something antipathetical to the Lord of the sixth." [Let your medicine be herbs in opposition to the planet ruling your sixth house. Thus, if Mars rules your sixth house, you might utilize herbs ruled by Venus.]

3. "If the Lord of the tenth be strong, make use of his medicines." [If the planet ruling your tenth house is elevated in the horoscope or is receiving many tight aspects, utilize herbs governed by this planet.]

4. "If this cannot be well, make use of the medicines of the Light of Time." [If you cannot use any of the above, then use herbs that have proven beneficial over a period of time.]

5. "Be sure always to fortify the grieved part of the body by sympathetical remedies." [Strengthen the weak parts of your body by herbs which work on those systems. For example, if you have weak lungs or respiratory difficulties, use mullein, coltsfoot, marshmallow root and similar herbs to work on this system.]

6. "Regard the heart, keep that upon the wheels, because the Sun is the foundation of life; and therefore those universal remedies *aarum potabile* and the Philosopher's stone cure all diseases by fortifying the heart." [Pay attention to the heart because it is the basis of life, and use remedies such as gold and the Philosopher's stone in addition to the specific herbal remedies.]

Culpeper recommended using herbs ruled by the planet opposite the one causing the disease. Thus, for diseases of Jupiter, use herbs of Mercury and the contrary; for diseases of the Luminaries, use the herbs of Saturn and the contrary; and for diseases of Mars, use the herbs of Venus and the contrary. Culpeper determined these opposite planets by using the old rulerships of the signs where planets rule two signs each:

fire masculine Leo	SUN MOON	Cancer feminine water
earth feminine Virgo	MERCURY	Gemini masculine air
air masculine Libra	VENUS	Taurus feminine earth
water feminine Scorpio	MARS	Aries masculine fire
fire masculine Sagittarius	JUPITER	Pisces feminine water
earth feminine Capricorn	SATURN	Aquarius masculine air

Taking the opposite sign:

Aries—Mars	Libra—Venus
Taurus—Venus	Scorpio—Mars
Gemini—Mercury	Sagittarius—Jupiter
Cancer—Moon	Capricorn—Saturn
Leo—Sun	Aquarius—Saturn
Virgo—Mercury	Pisces—Jupiter

In general, I tend to work with herbs corresponding to the rising sign and ruling planet for building and fortifying the body. For any health problems, I recommend herbs corresponding to the planet associated with that organ. For example, for lung problems I would consider Mercury and Gemini and herbs related to the respiratory system.

In order to get some idea of how herbs relate to the astrological signs and planets, I have grouped them accordingly. Some herbs fall into several of these groupings, but I have placed them in only one. Since there are so many herbs, I have chosen to categorize only the most common ones that are in general use. *Herbs listed under each sign do not mean that they are good for those with that particular Sun sign or Moon sign.* They simply have the vibration or qualities of the sign or ruling planet and may be helpful for those who have certain aspects to that planet or to planets in that sign natally, as well as during transits.

ARIES

Herbs ruled by the planet Mars and associated with Aries often have thorns, spines, or prickles. Thus, thistles and nettle, which is also referred to as stinging nettle, is included here. Thistles have many uses; blessed thistle and milkvane thistle work to balance the female reproductive system and are thus associated with the sign Scorpio. Herbs ruled by Mars are often red in color (cayenne, red clover, sassafras) and have stimulating effects. Aries herbs include the blood purifiers, herbs that are high in iron, and herbs that stimulate the adrenal glands. Some of these herbs are useful for those with the Sun, Moon, or Ascendant in Aries with hard aspects to Saturn or Neptune or for those with hard aspects between Mars and the Sun, Saturn or Neptune.

1. **Nettle**—The leaves of this plant are used as a tea for bleeding and anemia and as a blood purifier. Nettle is rich in iron, silicon, and potassium. The tea is also used as an expectorant for the lungs. For asthma, it is often combined with comfrey, mullein, horehound and a pinch of lobelia. Externally, nettle powder may be used on a wound to stop bleeding. Juice from nettle leaves can also be used for this and for hair growth when applied to the scalp. A poultice of nettle leaves is good for rheumatic pain. The tea, a diuretic used for gravel in the kidneys, is also used for diarrhea, dysentery, piles, and hemorrhoids.

2. **Burdock Root**—Burdock provides an abundance of iron, which makes it of special value as a blood purifier. It is used in this capacity for the treatment of arthritis, rheumatism, sciatica, and lumbago. It is also used to promote kidney function and works through the kidneys to help clear the blood of harmful acids. The diaphoretic property of burdock is due to a volatile oil, which when taken internally is eliminated from the sweat glands, thus removing toxic wastes. Sweating has a cooling effect on the body, so burdock is used to clear fevers and heat conditions as boils, sties, canker sores, and infections. Burdock seeds made into a tincture or extraction are good for skin and kidney diseases. Burdock can also be used as a fomentation for wounds, swellings, and hemorrhoids.

3. **Cayenne**—Cayenne powder, taken in water or juice or added to soups or salads, stimulates the heart and circulation. Cayenne is a preventative for heart attacks, flu, colds, indigestion, and lack of vitality. Cayenne powder will stop bleeding internally and externally. Cayenne is an excellent source of bioflavonoids, or vitamin P.

4. **Red Clover**—The blossoms of the plant are used. Red clover is an excellent blood purifier and can be combined with yellow dock, dandelion root, and other blood purifiers. It is also a good remedy for cancerous growths and has been used in formulas for getting rid of tumors. In salves, it is good for skin afflictions. As a gargle, it can alleviate throat swellings and infections.

5. **Gotu Kola**—The leaves of the plant are used primarily as a tea. Gotu kola is known to increase longevity and serves as a nerve tonic. It is good for depression, loss of memory, schizophrenia, and epilepsy. It is also a blood purifier and cools the blood; thus, it is of great value for fevers and inflammations. It is one of the most widely used herbs in Ayurvedic medicine.

6. **Fo Ti**—Fo ti, or fo ti tieng, is a Chinese root is used for longevity. (It is often referred to as the "elixir of life.") It is an excellent detoxifier; it builds healthy lung tissue; it is helpful in cases of low blood pressure; it relieves pains in rheumatism, arthritis, and gout. Fo ti is also used for certain eye and kidney problems, to lower blood sugar in diabetes, and to clear up hives and other allergic conditions.

7. **Sassafras**—The bark of sassafras is a strong blood purifier. It also stimulates and cleans the liver of toxins. It is used for menstrual problems, for pain after childbirth, and for eruptive skin conditions.

8. **Yellow Dock**—The root of yellow dock is high in iron and is used in the treatment of anemia. It is also an astringent blood purifier and is good for skin infections, tumors, liver, and gallbladder problems. It stimulates the flow of bile and is therefore a good laxative. As a salve, it is used to treat skin diseases and swelling.

9. **St. John's Wort**—St. John's Wort is an excellent blood purifier and is used for dysentery, jaundice, uterine pain, and diarrhea. The tea is also good for nervous conditions, like insomnia, and uterine cramps, but it should be used cautiously. The extracted oil is a beautiful shade of dark red and is a fine external application for burns, wounds, bruises, and other skin problems.

10. **Yarrow**—Externally, yarrow is applied to wounds to stop bleeding. As a tea, it is excellent for shrinking hemorrhoids, hemorrhages,

and bleeding of the lungs. It helps with menstrual cramps and stops excessive menstrual bleeding. For piles or vaginal secretions and hemorrhage, it is used as an enema or douche. The tea is also good for colds, flu, measles, and skin eruptions. Because of its tannins and essential oils, it makes a good antiseptic.

TAURUS

Herbs ruled by the planet Venus often have beautiful flowers and pleasant smells. Taurus herbs are soothing to the throat and its mucous membranes. They are also helpful for the colon, ruled by Scorpio, the polar opposite of Taurus. These herbs may be needed by those with the Sun, Moon, or Ascendant in Taurus with hard aspects to Saturn, Neptune, or Pluto; by those with hard aspects between Venus and Mars, Saturn, or Pluto; or by those experiencing transits of Saturn and Pluto to Venus.

1. **Licorice**—The root of licorice contains hormones similar to the adrenal cortical hormones; it is therefore helpful in treating adrenal insufficiency and other glandular problems. It induces the adrenal cortex to produce large amounts of cortisone and aldosterone. Licorice is also good for hoarseness and throat problems; it works for flu, colds, and lung congestion and is often added to cough syrups. Licorice root should be avoided for those with hypertension and hyper adrenal functioning.

2. **Slippery Elm**—The bark of the plant is used and often made into a powder. Slippery elm is beneficial for inflamed lungs and for treating bronchitis, coughs, and sore throats. It is often combined with licorice. Slippery elm heals stomach and intestinal ulcers and normalizes bowel function to relieve constipation and diarrhea. It makes an excellent food whenever there are problems with digestion. Since slippery elm is mucilaginous, it makes a good binder.

3. **Fenugreek**—Fenugreek tea (made from ground seeds) is excellent for sore throats and fevers. It is also good for mucus conditions of the lungs and for gas, ulcers, and diabetes. Externally, it can be used as a fomentation for boils, sores, and dry skin problems.

GEMINI

Herbs ruled by the planet Mercury have fine or divided leaves or stems (as grasses) and subtle odors. The herbs of Gemini strengthen the lungs and respiratory system; some are nervines that relax the nervous system. These herbs might be particularly useful for those with the Sun, Moon or the Ascendant in Gemini or those with hard aspects from Saturn, Uranus, Neptune, or Pluto to their Gemini planets or to Mercury.

1. **Coltsfoot**—The leaves of coltsfoot are used as an expectorant; it is a good cough medicine and is used for bronchitis, asthma, whooping cough, and other respiratory problems, often used in combination with horehound and marsh mallow. Coltsfoot is soothing to the stomach and intestines when there is inflammation and bleeding.

2. **Lobelia**—Lobelia, an antispasmodic, is used for the lungs and nervous problems. In small doses of the tincture (5–10 drops), it will act as a stimulant; in large doses—(1 t–1 T), it will act as a sedative. It is a good herb to add to cough medicines but should be used cautiously as it causes many to vomit. Externally, it is used as a wash for itchy skin diseases. It is added to liniments for sore muscles, pains and rheumatism. In large doses, it is used as an emetic.

3. **Mullein**—Mullein leaves are smoked to relieve congestion of the lungs. They are also used in tea combined with yerba santa and other herbs. The tea is good for lymphatic congestion, as well as diarrhea and intestinal problems, due to its mucilaginous quality that is very soothing to the body's linings. Mullein flowers are used as a nervine and antispasmodic. Oil made from mullein is one of the best remedies for ear infections.

4. **Horehound**—Horehound is a slightly bitter root that is effective for breaking up colds, expectorating mucus, and treating bronchitis and bronchial catarrh. It is made into a syrup for children. Taken hot, it will increase perspiration. Taken cold, it is a bitter digestive tonic.

5. **Yerba Santa**—The leaves of yerba santa are used in herbal smoking mixtures along with coltsfoot and mullein for bronchial spasms. Since lung congestion is often caused by digestive problems where excess mucus builds up in the intestinal tract, yerba santa stimulates

the digestive juices, improving digestion and correcting lung congestion. It is also used for diarrhea and dysentery.

6. **Hyssop**—Hyssop leaves are made into a tea for lung ailments, especially chronic catarrh. It is also a strong expectorant used for coughs and congestion from colds and flus. Hyssop is used to reduce fevers and improve digestion.

7. **Elecampane**—The root of elecampane is used in respiratory disorders like asthma and bronchitis and in catarrhal conditions of the nose and throat. The tea also stimulates digestion and is a wash for skin infections. For chronic lung ailments, it is often combined with wild cherry bark, pine bark, comfrey root, and licorice.

8. **Lemon Balm**—Lemon balm is a soothing tea for the nerves and good for colds, flus, and fevers. It is often combined with catnip and given to children when they are hyperactive. Mixed with elder flowers and spearmint, it alleviates colds and flus.

CANCER

Herbs ruled by the Moon often have soft juicy leaves and contain a lot of moisture. Cancer herbs are soothing to the stomach and aid digestion. They are helpful for those who have their Sun, Moon, or Ascendant in Cancer with hard aspects to Mars, Saturn, or Uranus as well as for those who have Saturn or Mars in Cancer.

1. **Peppermint**—Peppermint tea is good for gas, vomiting, nausea, diarrhea, and dysentery. This strong stimulant relieves chills and fever. As an antispasmodic, peppermint is good for spasms and convulsions in infants; it is also used for griping pains in the intestines. Peppermint oil, breathed in through the mouth and sinuses, will open up the nostrils.

2. **Spearmint**—Spearmint is a soothing tea for the stomach with mild diuretic properties. It is used for colds, flu, indigestion, cramps, gas, and spasms. It is also used to flavor more bitter teas. Peppermint is a strong stimulant, but spearmint is also used as a nervine herb.

3. **Papaya Leaf**—Papaya leaf tea aids digestion and is comforting to the stomach and intestines. It is helpful for intestinal cramps and gas and can be used instead of enzyme tablets.

LEO

Some herbs and plants under the rulership of the Sun have a golden orange color, are large in size, and have a radiating shape (as the sunflower). Herbs of Leo strengthen the heart, regulate blood pressure, and may also have an uplifting effect on the spirit (as borage). These herbs may be called for by those who have the Sun, Moon, or Ascendant in Leo in hard aspect to Saturn, Uranus, Neptune, or Pluto and by those who have Saturn in Leo with hard aspects to Mars, Uranus, Neptune, or Pluto.

1. **Borage**—Borage leaves make an excellent tea for strengthening the heart. Borage is also good for lung problems and reducing high fevers. It contains much magnesium, which is important for the heart and nervous system. Externally, borage is used for irritations of the skin and mucous membranes in salves and liniments.

2. **Hawthorn**—Hawthorn berries are used to treat high and low blood pressure, rapid or arrhythmic heartbeat, inflammation of the heart muscle, and arteriosclerosis. Using it regularly strengthens the heart muscle. Hawthorn is also useful for relieving insomnia, and a decoction of the berries is good for treating a sore throat.

3. **European Mistletoe**—European mistletoe is used as a cardiac tonic and a circulation stimulant. At first, it will raise the blood pressure, then lower it. The extract is a good cure for arteriosclerosis. Mistletoe may be cooked with hawthorn berries and wild leeks and drunk as a broth three times daily. It's also beneficial for dizziness, vertigo, and headaches. Do not eat the berries. (Be sure it is European mistletoe as U.S. mistletoe is toxic.)

4. **Motherwort**—Motherwort is a good heart tonic combined with hawthorn berries. It is used to treat palpitations and to prevent heart attacks. Motherwort is also useful for suppressed menstruation and other female complaints when combined with cramp bark and squawvine. A hot fomentation will relieve cramps and pain during menstruation. It is excellent for nervous conditions as hysteria, convulsions, and insomnia.

VIRGO

Herbs under the sign Virgo aid digestion and are carminatives (expel gas). Also included are herbs that are high in potassium. (The cell salt kali sulph, or potassium sulphate, is the Virgo salt.) These herbs may be helpful for those who have the Sun, Moon, or Ascendant in Virgo in hard aspect to Mars, Saturn, Uranus, Neptune, or Pluto; Mars in Virgo with hard aspects to Saturn, Uranus, Neptune, or Pluto; or Saturn in Virgo with hard aspects to Mars, Uranus, Neptune, or Pluto.

1. **Blackberry**—The leaves and root bark are used. The leaves made into an infusion are a good remedy for milder cases of diarrhea and sore throats. The root simmered (often with one teaspoon of cinnamon powder) is excellent for stronger cases of diarrhea, dysentery, and intestinal upset.

2. **Dill**—Dill seeds are excellent for aiding digestion and intestinal problems. They are often ground up with fennel and anise seeds and then simmered with a few cups of water.

3. **Fennel**—Ground-up fennel seeds or a few drops of the fluid extract or oil of fennel are used for treating gas, acid stomach, colic, and cramps. Fennel also increases the flow of urine, menstrual blood, and mother's milk.

4. **Flax**—Flax seed has strong mucilaginous qualities, which makes it good for all intestinal inflammations. Tea can be made from the seed or it can be ground up and taken in juice, cereal, or soups. The tea is also good for coughs, asthma, and pleurisy. Mixed in poultices with slippery elm, it is a good remedy for sores, boils, carbuncles, inflammations, and tumors.

5. **Plantain**—The leaves of plantain are soothing and effective in treating diarrhea, hemorrhoids, inflammations, ulcers, and bronchitis. Since plantain is high in potassium, it neutralizes stomach acids. The seeds of plantain (known as psyllium seeds) are a good bulk laxative. Soaked overnight in water, the seeds will produce a gel, which can be boiled, pressed through a strainer, and used for ulcers and intestinal pains. Plantain is also a good diuretic; the wider the leaves, the more pronounced the diuretic effect. Plantain leaves,

moistened and applied to the skin, relieve the pain and neutralize the toxins of insect and snake bites. Plantain is also used in salves and ointments, along with chickweed, comfrey, and elder flowers, for skin infections and chronic skin problems.

LIBRA

Herbs under the sign Libra help to balance the kidneys and bladder; they are also good diuretics (increase the flow of urine). These herbs are useful for those with several planets in Libra; the Sun, Moon, or Ascendant in Libra in hard aspect to Mars, Saturn, Uranus, Neptune, or Pluto; or Mars, Jupiter, or Saturn in Libra with hard aspects to the other outer planets.

1. **Cleavers**—Cleavers is a powerful diuretic and is used for all kidney and bladder problems, especially obstructions of the urinary organs such as stones and gravel. It is useful for treating edema, skin diseases, and eruptions. It cleans the blood and strengthens the liver. Externally, it is used in a salve for scalds and burns. It should be used fresh or it has little value.

2. **Corn Silk**—Corn silk leaves are made into a tea to treat irritated kidney and bladder conditions. Corn silk removes gravel from the kidneys, bladder, and prostate gland. It is an excellent remedy for all inflammatory conditions of the urethra, bladder, prostate, and kidneys.

3. **Juniper**—Juniper berries are a stimulating diuretic, but in large doses they can be irritating. They are beneficial in the treatment of urine retention, gravel, bladder discharges, and uric acid buildup. They are also useful in treating indigestion and flatulence.

4. **Parsley**—Parsley leaves help alleviate bladder infections, especially when combined with equal parts of echinacea and marshmallow root. Parsley leaves are best taken in salads or juiced. The root is good for treating ailments of the liver and gallbladder. It is also used for water retention, asthma, and jaundice. Parsley is high in chlorophyll and has been used for treating cancer as well as nervous problems where a high content of magnesium is required. (Chlorophyll contains the magnesium ion.)

5. **Prince's Pine**—(Pipsissewa) When made into a tea, the leaves of prince's pine are a good remedy for urinary and genital infections. It is similar to uva ursi, though somewhat milder. Pipsissewa is used for the treatment of skin diseases resulting from faulty elimination. It is beneficial for arthritis and rheumatism and tends to tonify the organs while providing a mild laxative effect.

6. **Uva Ursi**—The leaves of uva ursi infused as a tea are specifically for nephritis, cystitis, and kidney and bladder stones. It is best when combined with other diuretics and marshmallow, which has a mucilaginous quality. Uva ursi is astringent, tonic, and good for chronic diarrhea, dysentery, and profuse menstruation.

7. **Buchu Leaves**—Buchu leaves are one of the best diuretics. They are used for both acute and chronic bladder and kidney disorders including inflammation of the urethra, nephritis, and cystitis. As with most diuretics, buchu works best when taken cold. It is commonly combined with uva ursi in treating water retention and urinary tract infections. Used warm, it helps treat enlargement of the prostate gland and irritations of the membrane of the urethra.

SCORPIO

Herbs ruled by Pluto are often found in remote places and under the ground (certain roots). Scorpio herbs balance the hormones and aid in regulation of the menstrual cycle, childbirth, and pregnancy. Also included are herbs that are soothing and mucilaginous to the colon, aiding elimination. These herbs may be called for by those with the Sun, Moon, or Ascendant in Scorpio with hard aspects to Mars, Saturn, Uranus, Neptune, or Pluto; and by those with Mars or Saturn in Scorpio with hard aspects to the outer planets.

1. **Black Cohosh**—Black cohosh was used by Native American women to relieve pains from menstruation and childbirth. It is a good antispasmodic for all nervous conditions, cramps, and pain. Along with equal parts of elecampane, wild cherry bark, and yerba santa, it is an excellent remedy for whooping cough, asthma, and bronchitis (in capsules, tincture, or syrup). It is also used for high

blood pressure and to equalize circulation. This is a very potent herb, and an overdose will produce nausea and vomiting.

2. **Blue Cohosh**—Blue cohosh was also used among the Native American women for menstrual pains and childbirth. It was taken during the last month of pregnancy to aid in a painless delivery. Often it is combined with black cohosh because the herbs have complementary properties in producing an antispasmodic effect on the entire system. It is used with other herbs to treat bronchitis, nervous disorders, and rheumatism.

3. **Aloe Vera**—Taken internally, aloe vera regulates the bowels and has a laxative effect. It is also cleansing for the liver and kidneys. It is often used with ginger or fennel tea to prevent griping. Externally, the gel is used on the skin for burns, skin rashes, and irritations.

4. **Blessed Thistle**—Blessed thistle or milkvane thistle is noted for increasing mother's milk when taken with equal parts of red raspberry leaves and marshmallow root. It is used in formulas for menstrual cramps and problems. It is also an excellent tonic for the stomach, liver, and heart, increasing circulation.

5. **Cascara Sagrada**—Cascara is used as a laxative and tonic to the colon. It is generally taken as a tincture or in capsules due to its bitterness. It can help with hemorrhoids as well. To prevent griping, it may be used with anise or fennel seeds. Cascara is also stimulating to the liver, gallbladder, stomach, and pancreas and increases their secretions. The herb must be aged to be effective.

6. **Cramp Bark**—Cramp bark relieves menstrual cramps; it is usually combined with equal parts of ginger and angelica root and three parts chamomile for cramps and convulsions. It is also used for heart palpitation, rheumatism, and asthma.

7. **Dong Quai Root**—Dong quai is a Chinese herb used for most female ailments. It treats menstrual cramps, irregular menstrual cycles, and menopause. It is also an antispasmodic for treating insomnia, hypertension, and cramps. Dong quai is a good blood purifier and is used in treating anemia as well as warming the circulation.

8. **Ginseng**—Another Chinese herb, ginseng is well known for providing energy to the body and for rejuvenating and toning. It is used to normalize blood pressure, reduce blood cholesterol, and prevent atherosclerosis. It reduces blood sugar levels and thus is helpful in diabetes. Since it is a very yang herb, it should not be used in any conditions where there is heat or inflammation.

9. **Pennyroyal**—The leaf is used in a tea to regulate the menstrual flow and relieve cramps. It has been used to induce abortions, but serious problems have often arisen, especially when the oil is used for this purpose. Pennyroyal is also good for lung infections and fevers (driving out the heat through the pores of the skin) and circulation. Since it is a strong-smelling mint, it is used externally to repel insects and flies.

10. **Raspberry Leaf**—Raspberry leaf tea is a wonderful toner for the female organs. It is used throughout pregnancy for relieving nausea as well as easing cramps and pain in childbirth. It is also used to reduce menstrual cramps and regulate the female cycle. Raspberry leaf is combined with other herbs as uva ursi and squawvine to treat vaginal discharge and other female disorders.

11. **Senna**—Senna leaves and pods are used as a laxative since they increase peristaltic movements of the intestinal tract. Senna is best combined with a carminative like fennel, anise, coriander or ginger, to prevent cramping.

12. **Saw Palmetto Berries**—Saw palmetto berries are valuable in treating diseases of the reproductive organs, ovaries, prostate, and testes. This is one of the major herbs used for prostate problems. It is also useful for throat difficulties, colds, bronchitis, and whooping cough.

13. **Squawvine**—Squawvine was used by American Indian women as a tea during pregnancy to assure the proper development of the child, make the delivery safe, and help develop proper lactation. It is excellent for painful and irregular menstruation and relieves congestion in the ovaries and uterus. It is often combined with raspberry leaf. If the berries are crushed and added to a tincture of myrrh

for a few days, then strained, it will provide a good fomentation for sore nipples. It is also a good diuretic and can be used for gravel or kidney and bladder complaints.

14. **False Unicorn**—False unicorn is used in the treatment of female sterility and impotence. It is also used for amenorrhea, irregular menstruation, and leukorrhea. To strengthen female fertility and prevent miscarriage, it may be taken daily for several months. It is often combined with other herbs like cramp bark.

SAGITTARIUS

Herbs ruled by the planet Jupiter tend to be large in size and fairly conspicuous; they are usually quite nutritious (as dandelion root) and have a pleasant odor. The herbs of Sagittarius are good for the liver, increasing bile flow, and work with the pancreas in balancing the metabolism. Sagittarius also rules herbs high in the mineral silica. These herbs are often needed by those with a Sagittarius Sun, Moon, or Ascendant in hard aspect to Jupiter or Neptune; Mars in Sagittarius with hard aspects to Jupiter or Neptune; Jupiter in Sagittarius with hard aspects to Saturn, Uranus or Neptune; or Saturn in Sagittarius with hard aspects to Neptune.

1. **Dandelion**—The root and leaf of this herb are used, making one of the strongest liver medicines. Dandelion root detoxifies the liver and is a blood purifier. It has helped to clear up serious cases of hepatitis. It is also useful for cleansing the spleen, pancreas, gallbladder, bladder, and kidneys. In both diabetes and hypoglycemia, dandelion root has proved beneficial. The root contains a high content of easily assimilable minerals. It helps to lower blood pressure, thus aiding the action of the heart. The roasted roots are used for a coffee substitute along with chicory, which has similar properties. Dandelion leaves are a good diuretic and an excellent source of minerals; they can be used fresh in salads.

2. **Horsetail**—Horsetail (also known as shavegrass) is a reliable diuretic and is used for all urinary disorders. It is extremely rich in minerals, especially silica and selenium. Fractured bones have healed much faster when horsetail has been used. It is also helpful

for arthritis and rheumatism. Horsetail helps coagulate blood and thus is used to stop bleeding. Excessive use irritates the kidneys and intestines, so it is best used over a short period of time. It makes an excellent scouring brush since it is ridged with silica.

3. **Mandrake**—The root of mandrake is a powerful herb that should only be used in small doses. It is used for the treatment of chronic liver disease, bile imbalances, skin eruptions, lymphatic problems, and digestive troubles. It is best in combination with ginger, licorice root, or Oregon grape root. Externally, the tincture boiled down and concentrated is used for warts and as a wash for skin diseases.

4. **Oregon Grape Root**—Oregon grape root stimulates the production of bile and purifies the blood. It is used in the treatment of skin diseases, hepatitis, and rheumatoid arthritis. Because it stimulates the liver and gallbladder, it is helpful in overcoming constipation. Oregon grape root is similar to barberry root, but it has a stronger effect on the thyroid gland.

5. **Wild Yam**—Wild yam stimulates the bile and thus is beneficial to the functioning of the gallbladder and liver. It is an important ingredient in glandular balancing formulas and in female formulas because it contains natural estrogen. It is also a valuable antispasmodic to alleviate griping, menstrual cramps, and muscle spasms in addition to treating arthritis and joint inflammation. Wild yam is used in small quantities as a tea or capsules.

CAPRICORN

Herbs ruled by the planet Saturn may have few flowers, an unpleasant smell or taste, and may be poisonous (as hemlock and nightshade). Herbs under the sign Capricorn are high in calcium and useful in treating arthritis and rheumatism, broken bones and teeth. These herbs may be helpful for those with the Sun, Moon, or Ascendant in Capricorn with hard aspects to Mars, Saturn, Uranus, or Neptune and for those who have Saturn in Capricorn with hard aspects to Mars, Uranus, or Neptune.

1. **Comfrey**—Comfrey root and leaf is one of the most useful and versatile herbs. Internally, it is used to stop bleeding, to help the

pancreas in regulating blood sugar levels, and to promote the secretion of pepsin and thus aid digestion. Its mucilaginous properties, especially of the root, have been used to treat lung problems, coughs, and intestinal problems. Comfrey is also helpful for fractures because of its high content of calcium and magnesium. Externally, it is used in salves and as a poultice.

2. **Sarsaparilla**—Sarsaparilla root is used in treating rheumatism, arthritis and gout, as well as colds and fevers. The hot tea is a good diaphoretic for fevers. It is a strong blood purifier and is frequently combined with sassafras and yellow dock. It also contains hormone-like substances and is valuable in formulas for glandular balancing and for menopause and irregular menstruation. Externally, it is used for the treatment of skin problems and as an eyewash.

3. **White Oak**—White oak bark is an astringent used for ulcers, diarrhea, and problems with the spleen. It increases the flow of urine and helps remove gallstones and kidney stones. As a douche, it is good for vaginal infections. Externally, it is used for wounds and insect bites as well as poison oak and ivy. It is also applied to the gums to prevent tooth loss. A fomentation may be administered overnight to reduce swollen glands, mumps, and lymphatic swelling.

4. **Wintergreen**—Wintergreen contains salicylic acid, a good pain reliever for arthritis and rheumatism. It is also a good nervine and a carminative for relieving gas. Wintergreen oil rubbed into the body or in a bath or steam is extremely helpful for muscle or joint pain. Both willow and birch also contain salicylic acid and were used in a similar way by the Native Americans.

5. **Rue**—Rue is an antispasmodic herb used in the treatment of hypertension, neuralgia, and nervous problems. It is also used for strained tendons and muscles. As a tincture, it is used for sedation, rheumatism, increasing circulation, poor digestion, and gas. Externally, the fresh-bruised herb is used as a rubefacient to promote circulation and help sciatica.

AQUARIUS

Herbs ruled by Uranus grow in unusual places and may not always look the same. Herbs under the sign Aquarius are helpful for circulation and are also relaxing for the nervous system; they help to cool down the Uranian vibrations. These herbs are often called for by those with several planets in Aquarius or Gemini; the Sun, Moon, or Ascendant in Aquarius with hard aspects to Mercury or Uranus; or hard aspects between Mercury and Uranus or Mars and Uranus.

1. **Prickly Ash**—The bark of prickly ash is an excellent stimulant that increases warmth in the extremities and is used for arthritis and rheumatism. It is also a good blood purifier used for treating skin diseases and deposits in the joints. Prickly ash is warming to the stomach and is used for cramps and colic. For acute ailments, it is used as a stimulant in herbal formulas. Externally, prickly ash is applied as a poultice to help dry up wounds.

2. **Chamomile**—One of the most widely used herbs, chamomile is calming for restlessness, anxiety, nervous stomach, and insomnia. It is good for children in treating indigestion and nervous disorders. It helps relieve menstrual cramps as well. Externally, chamomile is applied to sore muscles and swellings.

3. **Catnip**—Catnip is another mild sedative useful for children. It is often mixed with chamomile, lemon balm, and spearmint. Catnip also cures diarrhea and is used in enemas to expel worms, release gas, and treat fevers.

4. **Passion Flower**—Passion flower is used for nervous conditions without pain like insomnia, restlessness, and nervous headaches. For children, it is good for muscle twitching and irritability. It also works for sciatica and nerve conditions of the aged.

5. **Scullcap**—Scullcap is used for chronic as well as mild nervous system problems. It helps individuals who are trying to wean themselves from barbiturates and valium. In combination with American ginseng, it is a good treatment for alcoholic withdrawal. It is a remedy for hysteria, neuralgia, epilepsy, and convulsions.

Scullcap is often combined with other tonic nervine and antispasmodic herbs as hops, passion flower, lady's slipper, and wood betony.

6. **Lady's Slipper**—Used as a tonic for exhausted nervous systems, lady's slipper improves circulation and nutrition of the nerves. It is used to treat cholera, hysteria, nervous headaches, and insomnia. It is combined with small amounts of ginger for fevers and pneumonia. With dandelion or chamomile, it curbs stomach and liver problems.

7. **Valerian**—Valerian is a strong sedative and nerve tonic. While it is sedating for all emotional disturbances and pain, it is used in many nervine formulas for its antispasmodic effect. As a bedtime tea, valerian is often mixed with hops. At first, valerian may seem to be a stimulant because the oil of valerian must be broken down by enzymes into valeramic acid before the sedative effect can be felt.

8. **Hops**—Like valerian, hops is a strong nervine and used for insomnia. It also tones up the liver and digestive tract, increasing the flow of bile. Hops is used for nervous stomach, gas, and intestinal cramps.

PISCES

Herbs ruled by the planet Neptune are difficult to find and may be deceptive in their effects. Under the sign Pisces are herbs that strengthen the immune system; some of them also have an antibacterial effect. A number of Piscean herbs catalyze heightened states of awareness. Some of these herbs may be particularly useful for those having Neptune transits; for those with the Sun, Moon, or Ascendant in Pisces square Neptune or Jupiter; and for those with hard aspects between Neptune and Mars, Jupiter, or Saturn.

1. **Golden Seal**—Golden seal is an herb that has many uses internally and externally. It is a good substitute for antibiotics and may be used for infection. It is also a good herb for the liver, especially as a tea made from golden seal leaf. When added to certain herbs, it increases the tonic properties of the organs being treated. It is used with eyebright as a tonic for the eyes, with gotu kola as a tonic for the brain, with squawvine as a tonic for the genito-urinary system in women, and with cascara bark as a lower bowel tonic. Small

doses may be used for morning sickness during pregnancy in combination with powdered cloves in gelatin capsules. It is excellent as a douche for vaginal infections, as an eyewash, and as a mouthwash for pyorrhea. It is used as a drink and gargle for tonsillitis and other throat problems. In combination with other herbs, especially myrrh, golden seal salve produces wonderful antiseptic effects. Excessive use of golden seal internally can diminish absorption of B vitamins because it reduces the favorable intestinal bacteria that influence the production and assimilation of these vitamins.

2. **Myrrh**—Myrrh gum is a powerful antiseptic. Used with golden seal in capsules or tea, it is good for intestinal ulcers, bad breath, catarrh of the intestines, and other mucous membrane conditions. The tincture added to water is an excellent mouthwash for spongy gums, pyorrhea, and throat infections. It is successful in treating chronic diarrhea, lung diseases, and general body weakness. Myrrh and other gums should be used in small amounts internally as they contain volatile oils that are toxic in large amounts.

3. **Chaparral**—Chaparral is one of the best natural antibiotics used internally and externally. It is good for treating bacterial, viral, and parasitic infections. It is also taken for inflammations of the intestinal and respiratory tracts and for urinary tract infections. Chaparral contains an antitumor substance called NDGA, which is a powerful antioxidant used in preserving fats and oils. The Native Americans used it to treat cancer. It is a very bitter herb and is usually mixed with other herbs as a tea. Externally, it is applied to wounds as an antiseptic, to the skin in the treatment of itching, eczema, and scabies, and to the scalp as a hair tonic and for dandruff.

4. **Echinacea Root**—Echinacea root is one of the very best herbal blood cleansers and lymphatic cleansers. It is used for blood poisoning, pus conditions, abscesses of the teeth, gangrene, lymph swellings, and snake and spider bites. It also breaks up congestion in the lungs and sinuses and is used for colds and flus.

5. **Eyebright**—Eyebright tea is used both internally and externally for the eyes, the liver, and detoxification of the blood. It aids the liver in cleansing the blood and relieves conditions that affect the

clarity of vision and thought. It is also used for inflammations of the nose and throat. Externally, the tea is used as an eyewash, often combined with golden seal, rue, or fennel for conjunctivitis, eye weakness, and other eye diseases.

6. **Mugwort**—Mugwort is known for its use in dream pillows to promote dreams and inner psychic states. It is also an excellent nervine for insomnia and shaking. The tea is good for stomach disorders but needs to be diluted to overcome the strong taste and concentrated action. It is also good for menstrual cramps, bronchitis, and fevers.

7. **Kava-Kava**—Kava-kava is a Polynesian herb whose root is ground up to make an infusion. It is a good remedy for insomnia and nervousness, and if used at night will bring about a deep sleep with clear dreams. It is also a potent analgesic taken internally or applied directly to a wound. In addition, it is used as a diuretic to treat urinary tract infections.

Planets and Signs and Their Relationship to Music and Color

Possibly the two oldest forms of healing on our planet are the use of music and color. Sound was present before humans were created. The Hindus believed the Universe was created from sound; they called the first sound Nada Brahma. Brahma, one of the three central gods in Hinduism, and Brahman come from the Sanskrit root *bri,* which means "to grow" but also "to praise"; everything that is growing and alive is Brahma. Nada Brahma means not only that God is sound, but Creation, the cosmos, the world is sound. Vibrations from sound create light and darkness as well as color. Ancient humans attuned to particular sounds that produced changes in mood.

In their healing ceremonies, primitive cults used songs and chants. The Native Americans are able to demonstrate that certain drum rhythms can cause rain, restore fertility, make the grass grow, and ripen corn.

Both Pythagoras and Pluto conceived of the universe as a musical instrument and wrote of "the harmony of the spheres". Pythagoras discovered the diatonic scale and the measurement of musical intervals. He found that all things, animate and inanimate, are constructed upon harmonic patterns whose ratios translate into basic chords. Johannes Kepler also wrote about the harmony of the spheres in relation to their orbits.

Historically, initiates like Orpheus and King David produced strong healings with their highly evolved spiritual music. In the early mystery schools, chants, mantras, and invocations were constructed to produce certain spiritual results. The temple priests determined the keynote of each pupil (each human being was keyed to one of the planets) and taught them how to attune to the corresponding planet (called the parent star) and to draw on the spiritual power of that planet. In the temples of Egypt, the keynotes of the seven planets were intoned. In Greece, the seven vowels of the Greek language were used as a channel for these planetary sounds. The Persians celebrated the entry of the Sun into each zodiacal sign with music, stressing the vibratory keynote of the presiding hierarchy at the time. Advanced initiates placed themselves in harmony with the music of their own particular sign and planet and received greater benefits.

The Greeks divided music into three parts—rhythm, melody, and harmony. Rhythm was associated with the physical life and the functions of the body; melody, with one's psychic being—emotional and mental; and harmony, with the totality of one's spiritual existence.

Primitive people depended heavily upon the influence of *rhythm*; the drum is one of the oldest musical instruments. Many tribes have more than 250 distinct drum rhythms. Primitive rhythms have a hypnotic effect, causing the body to vibrate in unison with the drum. This affects the rate of the heartbeat and influences the mind and emotions.

Melody is a succession of simple tones within a given harmonic (key) and rhythm structure; it is a sequence of musical sounds. The melodic line is strong in the religious music of the Near East; it is associated with the psychic nature and produced by the emotional pressures at the time. Anger was often expressed in a minor key, and other emotions found their own keys or frequencies.

Harmony is the combination of tones into a chord; the laws governing harmonic intervals are the ones discovered by Pythagoras. Orderly progression makes harmony possible; harmony implies the reconciliation of apparent differences on some level. Harmonic music contributes to the complete integration of the person and therefore is associated with wisdom and understanding. Health is dependent on the reconciliation of all parts of the being.

The roots of *music therapy* are ancient. Music has the tendency to bind individuals together. It was used by working people in all cultures as they performed some common work (like the rowing of boats). It was also used in religious worship by congregations of individuals to unite their energies. Today, music is used in industry to combat psychic fatigue—draining of energy, discouragement, low incentive, and depression. After World War II, music was used for battle fatigue; men who had lost all contact with objective existence did respond to carefully selected music. Doctors and dentists have used certain musical selections in their offices to relax patients and reduce apprehension.

Music therapy is being utilized to heal psychiatric patients and handicapped children. Dr. Paul Nordoff, an American composer, and Clive Robbins, a special educator working with handicapped children, used music therapy with autistic, mongoloid, and brain-damaged children. When working with children, the therapist improvises both vocally and at the piano to give them an expression of their mood—frustration, rage, anxiety. The child is encouraged to respond on percussion instruments, on the piano, or through the voice.

According to a research book edited by M. Critchley and R.A. Henson called *Music and the Brain: Studies in the Neurology of Music* (Charles C. Thomas, Pub. 1977), there are three neurophysiological processes that may be triggered by music. First, because music is nonverbal, it moves through the auditory cortex directly to the center of the *limbic system*, the mid-brain network that governs most of our emotional experiences as well as basic metabolic responses like body temperature, blood pressure, and heart rate. Second, music may be able to activate the flow of stored memory material across the *corpus callosum*, a collection of fibers connecting the left and right sides of the brain, helping the two sides to work in harmony. Third, music stimulates *endorphins*, natural opiates secreted by the hypothalamus that produce pleasure and a "high" feeling, like being in love.

In the 1930s the Swiss scientist Hans Jenny vibrated such inorganic matter as liquids, plastics, and powders atop metal disks. As he manipulated the pitch, the inorganic matter fashioned itself into various organic shapes. This discovery that sound could move inorganic matter into organic shape inspired British osteopath Peter Guy Manners to develop *cymatic therapy* in which sound is directly applied to the body for healing. Based on his theory that each part of the body vibrates at an audible frequency, Manners invented the cymatic instrument which transmits the "correct" frequency of health to a diseased organ. This treatment has been effective for neuromuscular problems as arthritis and degenerative bone conditions.

At the University of Massachusetts Medical Center in Worcester, patients can relax to Georgia Kelly's harp music broadcast over the Center's in-house television. The man who designed the program, Jon Kabat Zinn, leads patients through a session of breathing, relaxation, and positive affirmations with the music. Doctors at the Center have begun prescribing the program instead of tranquilizers for chronic pain.

Alfred A. Tomatis, a French doctor specializing in ear, nose, and throat problems, found that music was essential in providing life force to individuals. He was called to a Benedictine monastery where seventy of the ninety monks were totally exhausted, unable to work, and eating foods they had never desired. Discovering that the new abbot had eliminated six to eight hours of Gregorian chanting from the monks' schedule, Tomatis started them singing again and also hooked up each monk to headphones with baroque music. Within nine months, all but two of the monks were vigorously working and sleeping less. Tomatis believed that harmonious sound frequencies supply essential electrical charges to the brain.

Another modern form of music therapy is *toning*, originated by Laurel Keyes. The tone of a person's voice is indicative of their state of health; a whiny or gasping sound is an indication of being and feeling discouraged and hopeless, further drawing to themselves negative conditions by such sound. Another type of tone is that which carries hostility and resentment so that the individual constantly attracts Mars-like situations.

Toning involves a cleansing of the whole being and a tuning in to what one is really feeling and experiencing. It involves clearing out and opening the fifth chakra where we generate sound. To tone, one stands with eyes closed, relaxing the jaws and letting the sounds come out. One may groan or sigh or express feelings verbally. Toning stimulates the energy flowing in the body. (The phrase we use is "body tone".) One may do toning along with certain exercises like yoga or stretching.

Toning can also be done in groups for healing. One of the objectives of toning groups has been to send healing to those in need of it. The effects have been quite dramatic, and there are many case histories of those who have been healed through toning. A nurse who had been a diabetic with uremic poisoning and multiple sclerosis for years came to see Laurel Keyes with her sister. Laurel and the woman toned for the sister for 20 minutes, who experienced a real breakthrough of sobbing and understanding what was going on in her body. As she began to tone for herself, the uremic condition cleared up, her vision improved, and the multiple sclerosis was halted.

Musical prescriptions have been compiled by healers for various ailments. Compositions in different keys have different effects. The work of Sharry Edwards, an American healer, has been tremendously important in sound healing. Edwards is a clairaudient who is able to hear what sounds are missing in the individual's voice. After listening to the person speak, she sings the notes that are missing and makes a tape for them. This process has brought relief from many different kinds of symptoms.

In studying planetary vibrations, it has been found that the planets may chime. Seismographs revealed that the Earth rang with deep vibrations when the Chilean earthquake of 1960 sent oscillations throughout the sphere. These vibrations were too deep to be heard. If other planets also chime, they could radiate electromagnetic vibrations of low frequency across the void, inducing resonance and harmonies.

When *Voyager 2* drew close to Saturn, it picked up the whines and hisses of the magnetosphere and beamed them back to Earth. These were then speeded up and played through a music synthesizer, and the waves were found to consist of a kind of melody.

Johannes Kepler, a musician and astronomer, was the first to suggest that the orbits of the planets were elliptical. After this, it became apparent how precise the harmonic structure of the solar system was. In *Harmonium Mundi*, his most important work, Kepler showed that between the mutual velocities of the planets, there exists a great number of musical harmonies.

If planets do radiate tones to each other, their orbits, orbital speed, and distance from one another are important in determining harmonic results. *Bode's Law* explains their distances and the planets' orbits.

Johann D. Titius first discovered the law in 1766, but Johann Bode drew attention to it. Titius noticed that all of the planets known to astronomers had mean orbital distances from the innermost planet Mercury. These orbits became progressively greater by the ratio of 2:1 as they increased in distance from the Sun. Earth is twice as far from Mercury's orbit as Venus, Mars twice as far as Earth, etc. The ratio 2:1 is the ratio of the *octave*, and so the planets form a chain of octaves.

However, there was a gap in the chain; there existed no known planet between Mars and Jupiter, where, according to this law, there should be one. Then, in 1801, Giuseppe Piazzi discovered Ceres, a planetoid which orbited almost exactly where Bode's Law had predicted a planet should be. Later, other planetoids were discovered in the region, and the orbit became known as the asteroid belt. (The asteroids appear to be the remains of a former planet called Maldek which had been destroyed.) With the discoveries of Uranus, Neptune, and Pluto, it was found that Uranus and Pluto have mean orbits close to the exact distances necessary to complete two further octaves. Neptune is located halfway between Uranus and Pluto, filling in the half-octave position.

BODE'S LAW		
Planet	Perfect Octaves (Units of distance from Mercury)	Mean Orbits (Actual units of distance from Mercury)
Mercury	0	0
Venus	1	1.1
Earth	2	2
Mars	4	3.7
Asteroids	8	c. 8
Jupiter	16	16
Saturn	32	30.5
Uranus	64	62.6
Neptune	96	98.9
Pluto	128	130.1

These speeds on the harmonic level would represent the planets' pitch frequencies.

After Kepler's death, the three outermost planets were discovered—Uranus, Neptune, and Pluto. Since these planets have very low orbital velocities (it takes Pluto 248 years to go around the Sun), their transposition into sound would be below the human hearing capacity. Therefore, the orbital ellipses of the outer planets can be made audible to the human ear as rhythms because rhythms have lower vibrations than tones.

There exist many systems of assigning the signs to the various keys or notes of the octave. Here is one system for the signs given by Corinne Heline in her book, *Healing and Regeneration Through Music* (J.F. Rowny Press, 1968):

Aries—D major	Taurus—E major
Gemini—F major	Cancer—G major
Leo—A major	Virgo—C major
Libra—D major	Scorpio—E major
Sagittarius—F major	Capricorn—G major
Aquarius—A major	Pisces—B major

If the musical notes are included with their sharps and flats, they equal 12, the chromatic scale, and the number of the astrological signs and houses: do, re, re, mi, mi, fa, fa, so, la, la, ti, ti.

In recent years, it has become possible to make the sounds of the planets audible. Willie Ruff and John Rodgers of Yale University programmed the angular velocities of the planets into a synthesizer. Just as Kepler had computed it, they assigned the low G to the planet Saturn. Kepler's laws define the tones of all the other planets from Saturn to Jupiter, Mars, Earth, and Venus, to Mercury, which is the four line E-sharp, a note that is almost at the highest end of the piano keyboard. Ruff and Rodgers produced a record with these sounds of the planets. Mercury, the restless messenger, has a quick chirping sound. Aggressively, Mars slides up and down across several notes. Jupiter has a majestic tone, and Saturn has a low mysterious droning. The sound spectrum of the six visible planets, including Earth, covers eight octaves, almost identical with the human hearing range. Ruff and Rodgers used the outermost planets as rhythms in which Pluto became the bass drum. On their recording, Ruff and Rodgers realize as sounds the orbits of the planets for a time span of 250 years, beginning in 1571, the year of Kepler's birth. Their work was inspired by Hindemith's opera, *The Harmony of the World*, which was in turn inspired by the life and work of Johannes Kepler.

Michael Heleus, an American astrologer, has created a system called Astrosonics, which is a way to render the astrological chart as a vibration to be experienced. Astrosonics is much more, however, than just translating the astrological chart into sound. Astrosonics is a system of healing that uses planetary frequencies in various combinations to create particular emotional and psychological effects on individuals and the environment. Heleus works with the sacred geometry known to the ancients, which is based on the idea that every wavelength has its correlated frequency and idea. Sacred geometry was utilized in building the pyramids in Egypt, the Mayan pyramids, and in the ancient civilizations of India and China, which used the principles of cosmic resonance to surround themselves with particular vibrations. They also used them in their music; in this way they were cosmically connected to their environment. In an interview with Heleus (*Reconnecting with the Cosmic Bearings of Life Through the Right Use of Sound,* by Joe Landwehr, Whole Network Journal, Santa Fe, NM, summer 1988), Heleus mentions that the cathedral at Chartres has dimensions in its transept that relate directly with the motions of Jupiter, Saturn, and the Sun as seen from the Earth. This proves that this knowledge was also available in the Middle Ages.

Heleus explains the principle of Astrosonics by the example of imagining each planetary orbit as a long string that gets plucked. Each time you halve the length of the string, you double the frequency and raise the vibration one octave. If one does this thirty-odd times, the planet's orbital frequency becomes audible, and the sound produced invokes the characteristic of the planet's nature astrologically.

In practical terms, Heleus studies the client's astrological chart and determines certain planetary combinations that are related to the individual's symptoms—physiologically or psychologically. He then plays certain generic tapes (based on planetary combinations) to the client to see how the client experiences them—does the pain get better or worse, does the person feel calm or upset, etc. Heleus selects a couple of the generic tapes that he mails to the client along with at least one tape based on the personal horoscope. He first works with trines and sextiles in the chart since these are more easily accessible to the individual. Then he works with conjunctions, oppositions, squares, the more dynamic aspects. Heleus feels that "the generic sounds facilitate powerful changes on the higher levels while the personal sounds elicit a more personal connection to the work. Because the generic sounds are more impersonal and universal, they can at times be harder to relate to."

The way Heleus has categorized the planets according to their octaves is interesting. One octaval family is Mercury, Mars, Saturn, Pluto, and marginally Earth/Sun. This octave tends to have an association with analytical left-brain function. The other set—Moon, Venus, Uranus, Neptune, and marginally Jupiter, tends to have an intuitive right-brain function. He mentions that Neptune is literally an octave of Venus but lower, and that Pluto is fairly near an octave of Mars, also lower, but that Uranus is not at all an octaval relation of Mercury.

Heleus has developed many other generic tapes. One of these is of the solar phi chord, which creates an attunement to the motion of the Earth around the Sun and activates the crown chakra. When he used the solar phi chord, he found that it would help people coordinate the hemispheres of the brain. He has also developed a series of generic tapes that he calls "toward the Tao progressions." In these he creates a progression of sound based on polarities—yin/yang, light/dark. The progression takes one toward the yang part of the octave and then toward the yin part, and finally into a point of balance. These progressions help correct serious energy imbalances and can be powerful agents of change, according to Heleus. The Moon toward the Tao progression, for example, works on issues of emotional support, subconscious habit formation, compulsive behavior, and chemical dependency problems.

An example that Heleus gives is of a woman who felt cold all the time. She was in Michigan in the middle of winter, had just had her furnace fixed, and it was making a weird noise. He tested the sound and found that it was putting out an infrasound below the hearing threshold that was in resonance to a Saturn-Pluto opposition in her natal chart. This difficult aspect that she was being reminded of was putting her into a very cold psychological mode as well.

As in all other healing modalities, we have the opportunity to work with our sounds and move through various old patterns and conditionings that we carry in our being. Astrosonics can be one way of doing this. Heleus believes that Astrosonics is more powerful than simply working in the field of Psychoacoustics because Psychoacoustics takes into consideration the relationship between music theory, psychology, and physiology, but it has no grounding in astronomy or sacred geometry. Therefore, it gives us an egocentric or sociocentric basis of looking at things without the spiritual underpinnings.

Heleus also finds that Astrosonics synergizes very well with other avenues of healing, particularly subtle body work, flower essences, homeopathy, radionics, color therapy, and geometric therapy.

Another American astrologer, Gerald Jay Markoe, has formulated a system through which he translates a chart into a musical composition. An article about his work, "The Musical Correlations of a Natal Chart," was published in the NCGR bulletin Vol. 8, #34, Fall/Winter 1982.

Markoe translates the planets in the horoscope into a musical composition. He takes into consideration the speeds of the planets and whether a planet is rising, setting, or stationary. He works with harmonics—astrological and musical. The actual process relating planetary positions and music is highly complex and done by computer. The principle he uses is that each musical note corresponds to a mathematical ratio. For example, the note sol is found at 2/3 the length of a musical instrument string. Planetary positions also correspond to mathematical ratios. For example, the Sun can be 2/3 the way across the sky. At that moment, the Sun would be playing the note sol while the Moon and planets would each be playing their own notes, creating a celestial composition.

After the computer prints out the musical composition, it is recorded by Markoe on synthesizers and a Steinway grand piano. The astromusic tape begins with the notes for each planet played in zodiacal order, beginning at the Ascendant and then in order of their distance to the Earth. A "chorale" of the chords formed by various planetary groups is played, which reveals connections that may not be apparent in the chart. The music then goes on to explore the most beautiful note combinations, incorporating the discordant notes in relationship to the harmonious ones.

These examples of individual astrologer/musicians working with the horoscope through sound show how close the connections are between astrology and music and how important this combination can be as a healing modality.

Color

Color has been used since ancient times for producing specific psychological and emotional effects as well as for healing and balancing the body. Color is related to light and atmospheric density as its spectrum ranges from infrared (high density) to ultraviolet (low density). This spectrum follows the astrological signs, starting with Aries as red and ending with Pisces as violet. Sunlight, therefore, is important for healing since it contains all the colors of the spectrum.

Color is created by movement; this is referred to as the Doppler effect. The wavelength of light hitting Earth determines the color; if a star is moving away, it may appear red, a longer frequency; if it is moving toward us, it may appear blue since blue is a shorter frequency.

People who are deprived of light often suffer from many diseases that are physical, mental and emotional in nature, as well as visual deformities. In *The Principles of Light and Color* (Sun Publishing Co., 1898), Edwin D. Babbit M.D.

shares his observations on working with color and sunlight, which contains all the colors. When exposed to the Sun, the skin becomes darker, clearer, and more rosy. Dr. John Ott, in *Health and Light* (Pocket Books, Inc., 1973), describes the case of a photographer who nearly went blind from spending so much time in the darkroom.

Color was first isolated by Sir Isaac Newton, who established the presence of seven basic colors in the spectrum by admitting sunlight through a prism. Each of the seven colors has its own wavelength. The variations of the wavelengths are the distinguishing characteristic of the color. When the wavelengths become very short, they become invisible to the human eye, but the color may still exist (ultraviolet); similary for wavelengths longer than red (infrared).

People subjected to various colors experience mental and emotional changes as well as modifications in their muscular activity. Color is used to increase efficiency in industry, to help speed recovery in hospitals, and to assist concentration in schools.

Egyptian and Greek healing temples were painted various hues in order to have an effect upon worshippers. In Tibet, color rays were used as a tool in meditation.

In this century, Rudolf Steiner wrote about color treatments for various conditions, psychological and physiological. Dinshah P. Ghadali, a native of India, combined color therapy with sound and rhythm and invented a machine called the Spectro-chrome which beams various colors onto portions of the patient's body. He established the Spectro-chrome Institute in Malaga, NJ.

There are many forms of color healing. One can use the colors in foods for their nutritional benefits. Deep red foods as beets, dulse, and cherries contain iron. Green leafy vegetables are high in chlorophyll, which is the magnesium ion, and also contain many other essential minerals. Yellow foods as squashes and peaches can have a laxative effect. Drinking water in colored jars which have been placed in the sunlight is another way of getting the benefits from that particular color.

The essence of color healing consists of causing certain molecular reactions in the organism or vital centers through the medium of the rays. One of the simplest ways of doing color healing on various parts of the body is to use a lamp with color gels to focus any of the seven rays. There are two main kinds of ray treatment—*general diffusion* and *local concentration*. In general diffusion, the light rays are focused on the body, especially the back, the region of the spine and nervous system. This recharges the entire body and the nervous system. The patient sits or lies down, stripped to the waist, and is immersed in the light for 30 minutes. In local concentration, the light is focused only on the affected area. Light and color have a direct action on the protoplasm of the body and affect the speed of chemical reactions.

Other means of healing with color include placing colored glass in the windows of a room or in one's eyeglasses. Wearing clothes or gems of a particular color is a way of accenting that color in the aura. One of the best ways of color healing is through *color breathing*. Since air contains radiations from the Sun, stars, and planets, it contains all the colors of the spectrum. The color healer can practice deep rhythmic breathing with visualization of the rays. The first three rays, red, orange and yellow, are magnetic and should be visualized as flowing up from the Earth toward the solar plexus. The last three, blue, indigo and violet, are electrical and are breathed in from the ether downwards. The green ray, the balancer of the spectrum, flows into the system horizontally.

How to Use Color with the Horoscope
Color can be used to help balance the **elements**. Those who lack fire tend to need reds and oranges; lack of water calls for blues and pinks; earth, greens; and air, yellows. With an overabundance of fire, blue tones should be used; red balances an overabundance of water; violets and blue-violets for earth; and blues and greens for air.

In terms of the **qualities**, a lack of cardinal signs may need more red; lack of fixed, more green; and lack of mutable, more yellow. Excess cardinal energy calls for more blues and purples; fixed, more yellows; and mutable, more greens.

Working with **planetary color healing** is a way of using the planets and their color rays to balance out mental, emotional, and physical conditions. If a planet is weak in the natal horoscope, that color may be called for in a general sense and should be worn more often, as well as used in other forms of color healing. It may be that the particular planet is weakened at this time through a transit as, for example, Saturn making a hard aspect to Mars might deplete Mars energy and call for added reds and scarlets. Uranus transiting an important point in the horoscope may call for more blues to balance the nervous system. Neptune transits often open up our higher centers and we attune to violets and blue-violets. Pluto transits may catalyze us into some deep transformations where we feel the need to wear more white or black or sometimes purple.

Red and *scarlet* are related to the planet **Mars**. Red is a warm color and therefore a stimulant. It improves circulation and activates the nervous system which energizes all our senses. Used in cases of anemia, it increases the hemoglobin in the blood. It causes expulsion of toxins through the skin and may cause skin redness, itching, and rashes while the cleansing is in process. Red boosts the level of energy and increases aggressive tendencies. It engenders strength, courage, and enthusiasm. Red also works on the first chakra and can stimulate sexual energy.

Orange has an affinity with the planet **Saturn**. It is used to treat calcium deficiencies as well as to build bones. It is also a lung builder and respiratory stimulant. (In Oriental medicine, the lungs are related to depression, an interesting analogy to Saturn.) Orange is a digestive stimulant, relieving flatulence in the digestive tract. It energizes the thyroid and depresses the parathyroid. It helps the mammary glands to increase milk production and increases eliminative discharges, bringing boils and abscesses to a head. Orange is an antidote to repressions and limitations and inspires self-confidence and positive thinking. It is connected to the second chakra and is midway between red, which is allied to the physical body/first chakra, and yellow, which is allied to the mental body/third chakra. Orange is therefore important in the visualization of ideas. (Black was also associated with Saturn. In alchemy, Saturn was referred to as the "Sol Nigris," or Black Sun, because it had the ability to change color from black to orange.)

Yellow is a color related both to the **Sun** (in its golden hue) and to the planet **Jupiter** (because of its association with bile). Yellow stimulates the motor nervous system which energizes the muscles. It activates the production of bile, thus acting as a laxative. It also helps to increase the hydrochloric acid and pancreatic juices. Yellow depresses the spleen and is helpful in expelling worms. Yellow is a warming color and thus has been used to lift the spirits and to convey a sense of cheerfulness and warmth. It is connected with the third chakra or solar plexus which acts as the brain center of the nervous system. Yellow is associated with the mental body and works with the creation of thoughts and ideas.

Green is the color of the heart chakra and is midway between the warm end and the cool end of the spectrum, as the heart chakra is midway between the first and seventh. Therefore, it is the color of balance, harmony, and peace. Green is associated with the planet **Venus** and with the Earth. It is an extremely healing color and has been considered the master healer of the colors. (Venus is also the master healer in the sense that love breaks through all.) Since green is composed of yellow and blue, it influences the blood pressure and heart action. Green light provides the energy of the Sun in its safest and most natural form through plant energy known as chlorophyll, which is a high source of magnesium and an excellent medicine for the heart. It is also a fine tonic for tired nerves. Green denotes cooperation and thus has been used effectively in group situations. It is also the color of abundance and may be used to attract prosperity on all levels.

Turquoise has an affinity with **Venus** and also with **Jupiter** due to the associations of the turquoise stone with horses and rituals relating to Jupiter. (See the chapter on gems and crystals.) Turquoise is an excellent tranquilizer; it is cooling and relaxing and helps headaches and swelling. It is also a skin tonic and rebuilds burned skin. (The skin is ruled by Venus.) Since it has been used for so many centuries by Native Americans as a holy gem, it is associated with healing and peace.

Blue is related to **Mercury** and **Uranus**; it is an antidote of red due to its cooling qualities. It relieves itching and irritation and is used for fevers, fast pulse, and inflammatory conditions. The blue vibration raises the consciousness to the realm of spirit, so it is used in spiritual healing, meditation, and religious services. Blue has a soothing vibration and helps to heal and relax the nervous system. It is connected with the throat chakra and is also associated with artistic inspiration and wisdom.

Indigo, or blue-violet, is related to **Neptune**. The indigo ray is associated with the pineal gland, which influences the organs of sight, hearing, and smell. Indigo has an anaesthetic effect, making one insensitive to pain while being fully conscious. It is used to stimulate the parathyroid, depress the thyroid, purify the bloodstream, and treat convulsions and nervous ailments. It is also a mammary depressant. Indigo opens us to higher consciousness states and is associated with the third eye and psychism.

Violet is also related to **Neptune** and **Pluto**. Violet is the highest vibration of visible light, and its rays are stimulating to the nervous system. It arouses mysticism, spiritual intuition, and idealism. It restores mental equilibrium and appeals to sensitive people. It stimulates the spleen and promotes production of white blood cells. Violet helps to maintain the sodium/potassium balance in the body and is used for bladder trouble and overactive kidneys. It is a good remedy for neuralgia and mental disturbances; it induces deep relaxing sleep. Violet is connected with the chakra in the higher brain known as the pituitary gland, which is concerned with the spiritual intuitive faculty. This color aids the development of spiritual consciousness, clairvoyance, and psychic sensitivity. Its two divisions, purple and amethyst, correspond to the material and spiritual aspects.

Magenta or red-violet, is associated with **Pluto.** It is an important color for all heart disorders; it energizes the heart and stimulates the circulatory system and the adrenal glands, purifies the blood, and stimulates higher sexual energy. It also helps to dissolve kidney stones as well as regulate blood pressure and the arteries.

Black, which is the totality of all color, may be related to both **Saturn** and **Pluto. White** or *Silver* is related to the **Moon.** *Gold* is a form of yellow and is related to the **Sun.**

Colors and Rays
The seven major rays and their colors are as follows:

> Red—Life
>
> Orange—Energy
>
> Yellow—Intellect
>
> Green—Harmony and Empathy
>
> Blue—Religious Inspiration
>
> Indigo—Intuition
>
> Violet—Spirituality

The three primary colors red, yellow, and blue symbolize the three bodies.

1. The Physical Body (physical-etheric)

2. The Soul (astral-mental)

3. The Spirit (higher mental-spiritual)

From these evolve the secondary or complementary colors—orange, green, indigo, and violet.

The *aura* is the cohesive quantum energy field that creates the body and holds our emotions, thoughts, and behavior patterns in time and space. Energy flowing between different people as thoughts and feelings are actually moving between the auras of each individual. According to Barbara Brennan in her book, *Hands of Light* (Bantam, 1987), a "normal" or "quiet" aura has a dark blue-purple or clear layer pulsating out to one-quarter or one-half inch from the skin. It is constantly pulsating at the rate of about 15 pulses per minute. The pulsations form a wave-like motion down the arms, legs, and torso. The blue color turns to a yellow color around the head. When we have strong feelings, our "quiet" aura will be permeated by another color correlating to the emotional state we are experiencing. Someone who is angry may show pulsations of dark red in the aura, while someone speaking about their favorite topic may exhibit gold or silvery gold. Depression may be seen as dark gray and heavy, while fear has a whitish gray color. A person who is ill or who uses drugs or alcohol may exhibit "etheric mucus," or blockages in part of the aura.

The meanings of the colors in the aura are as follows:

Red—Clear bright red shows moving anger. Dark red shows stagnant anger. Red-orange indicates sexual passion, while rosy pink indicates pure unselfish love.

Orange—Bright clear orange shows health and vitality; deep orange, ambition.

Yellow—Golden yellow indicates high soul qualities; yellow in general shows intellectual prowess. An excess of yellow shows an abundance of mental power.

Green—Green denotes nurturing and healing. Dark muddy green shows envy. An excess of green may denote independence as well as healing ability.

Blue—Deep clear blue indicates a pure spiritual feeling; bright blue points to sensitivity and sincerity. An excess of blue signifies an artistic, harmonious nature and spiritual understanding.

Indigo—Indigo symbolizes moving toward a deeper connection with spirit.

Purple—Deep purple shows high spiritual attainment; lavender symbolizes spiritual consciousness.

White—Pure white indicates truth and purity.

Gold—Gold symbolizes connection to the divine, wholeness, and uplifted feeling.

Silver—Silver indicates deep communication.

Brown—Brown indicates practicality and earthiness; light brown, sensuality.

Black—Black indicates forgetting the self, thwarted ambition, depression, or invalidation.

Black Velvet—Black velvet indicates doorways to the Great Mystery, entering into the Unknown, transformation.

Gray—Gray indicates depression and sadness, and is the major color indicator of unconsciousness about specific issues in life.

Transits to our natal chart constantly change and transform our auric field. Sometimes these changes are temporary, as, for example, a day with Mars square our Mercury may make us restless and impatient. Our aura may show splotches of red shooting out, but these may be gone overnight. Long-term transits have different effects on the aura. Gray and black may be prevalent during a Saturn transit when we are feeling down and depressed. Indigo and often purple are in the aura during Neptune transits. These may become permanent as we connect deeper to our spiritual source. Uranus transits may cause the aura to change frequently, with many colors appearing and disappearing.

Color healing is extremely helpful in working with and learning to transform our transits. Using the color orange for Saturn transits works well to charge the vital and emotional energy. During Uranus transits, the color blue is very important for calming the nervous system; green also works well for balance, stability, and integration. Utilizing indigo, blue-purple, violet, and purple for Neptune helps us to reach our spiritual aspirations. Often rose and pink are helpful under Pluto transits if we are transforming old emotional patterns; green works well to bring out healing abilities and to nurture ourselves while we are going through Plutonian initiation.

Planetary Healing with Crystals and Gemstones

Crystals and gemstones have been used throughout the ages for their healing qualities. In ancient Egypt, the Ebers Papyrus recommended the use of certain astringent substances like lapis lazuli as ingredients for eye salves. Hematite, an iron oxide, was used for hemorrhages and reducing inflammation. Later, the potency of the gems was enhanced by engraving the images of certain gods and goddesses on them. In Rome, Pliny compiled material on gems, categorizing them by color and constitution as to which diseases they could cure. A distinction was made between the talismanic quality of stones for the cure and prevention of disease and the medicinal use of them as mineral substances. In the former case, they were simply worn on the person, while in the latter they were ground up in water or some other liquid.

Certain gemstones were prized for their planetary and spiritual vibrations. Stones were charged with the vibrations of the planets to make them more effective in healing. This was done at certain times of the day when the planet was on the horizon or during specific hours ruled by that planet. Gemstones were also charged at various times of the year; for example, a Scorpio stone may have been charged at the New Moon in Scorpio.

Engraving the stones with symbols or figures gave them more potency and made them into talismans for wearing on the body. In addition to the zodiacal signs and planets, the cross, ankh, pyramid, and Star of David were commonly used emblems.

Color symbolism was important in recommending certain stones for various disease states. Red stones such as the ruby, garnet, carnelian, and bloodstone were considered remedies for hemorrhage and inflammatory diseases. This was based upon the principle of like curing like. Yellow stones were prescribed for bilious disorders, jaundice, and other diseases of the liver. Stones of green hue relieved diseases of the eye due to the beneficial influence exerted by this color upon the sight. The lapis lazuli, sapphire, and other blue stones were believed to counteract the spirits of darkness and invoke the aid of the spirits of light and wisdom. Amethyst was said to counteract the effects of indulgence in intoxicating beverages.

Gemstones have been used for healing both externally and internally. Externally, they are worn directly on the body or in a setting of a precious metal such as gold or silver. They may be placed on the affected area of the body or on one of the chakras, or held in the hand and used on the area.

Internally, gemstones were used in a number of ways. In Europe, they were pulverized, and small amounts were mixed in wine or some other liquid and drunk. Ayurvedic physicians in India used the ashes of the gemstones (which had been pulverized) in preparing special medicines.

A less expensive way to use gems is to place the stone in liquid, usually a combination of alcohol and water, for several days and then drink the liquid. This liquid contains the vibration or essence of the particular stone. If this liquid is placed in the sunlight for several days, a tincture can be made from the gem, and it can be used as a mother tincture from which to make individual bottles of gem essences (similar to flower essences) for healing.

Crystals amplify energy and are used in ultrasound devices, watches, and memory chips in computers, in addition to being utilized for healing. The Mayans and other Native American tribes used crystals for diagnosis as well as for treatment of disease. Clear quartz crystals were used by the elders to foresee future events.

The different *shapes* of crystals are important in determining their healing properties. *Size* is also important as larger crystals carry more electromagnetic energy and are therefore more powerful. *Color* is important, too, in treating various ailments. For example, lavender crystals have been used in treating cancer, aqua for bone diseases, and green for internal organs, such as the liver, kidneys, and pancreas.

It is necessary to *cleanse* crystals before and after each healing. To do this, soak the crystal in purified water (not tap water) to which has been added one or two teaspoons of sea salt (available at health food stores). Let them soak overnight, or for a few hours at least. Crystals may also be cleansed by purifying them with the smoke of cedar, sage, or sweetgrass.

Crystals are often combined with other crystals in healing. Thus, four large quartz crystals may be positioned around a person while receiving a massage or other healing treatment, or a large crystal may be set under the table itself. Crystals may also be placed at the various chakric centers of the body, choosing a particular type of crystal that would benefit that area. A crystal may be worn in a pouch or medicine bag underneath the clothing next to the affected area of the body or close to one of the chakras or energy centers that is involved. It may also be made into a necklace or earrings for protection and to infuse the wearer with a certain desired vibration.

How to do a Crystal Healing

1. Prepare and cleanse the stones to be used.

2. Clear the room with sage or cedar, and then seal it off against outside influences. This can be done by placing clear quartz crystals in each corner of the room with their termination points toward each other.

3. Ground yourself using visualization of light traveling from the crown to the base of the spine. Feel the energy going into the Earth through the soles of the feet.

4. Discuss with your client where the blockages are—physical areas where there is constriction of emotional centers.

5. Have your client do some deep breathing and color visualization to attain a relaxed state.

6. Work on the constricted area with a clear quartz generator crystal, a wand, or your favorite heating crystal.

7. Choose (with the help of your client) appropriate crystals for each of the chakras. Place these on the chakras and have the person do some deep breathing to attune to each of the stones.

8. While the stones are on the chakric centers, have your client look at the area where there is constriction by going inside that area. The person may get a symbol or see a picture from childhood. This will lead to subsequent pictures and associations that should throw some light on the problem.

9. When the roots of the problem have been discovered, work on that area again with your healing crystal.

10. Then remove stones from each of the chakras, wiping them off with a cloth and setting them aside. Burn some sage or cedar to cleanse the atmosphere.

11. Help your client ground: provide some tea or water, and discuss the session.

12. Set up a maintenance program with affirmations and exercises.

Crystals and gemstones are mined just as other precious metals and minerals. Since they come from the Earth, they contain mineral constituents that provide them with their individual color and their healing properties. Some of the major mineral components of stones follow.

Silica—All quartzes and precious stones (except for diamond, rhodochrosite, and chrysoberyl) consist mostly of silicic acid, which dissociates into water and silica. Silica attracts light and drives out black forces. It promotes discharges of water from the body and protects the nerves. It also strengthens the back, imparting more self-confidence.

Magnesium—Found in olivine, serpentine, pyrope, and almandine. It strengthens the heart, relaxes the body, relieves cramps, and benefits the nervous system.

Manganese—Found in rhodochrosite, which consists entirely of manganese, rose quartz, amethyst, and almandine. It is good for paralysis and diseases of the nervous system as Parkinson's disease and is helpful for anemia.

Iron—Found in coral, bloodstone, ruby, garnet, magnetite, pyrite, and chlorite. It is important for inflammations, hemorrhage, and anemia.

Copper—Found in malachite, turquoise, chrysocolla, azurite, and pyrite. It strengthens the nerves, helps assimilate iron and relieves spasms and multiple sclerosis.

Calcium—Found in fluorspar, apatite, uvarovite, and andradite. It strengthens bones, nerves, teeth, and all structural elements of the body.

Chromium—Found in emerald, malachite, and uvarovite. It is necessary for the formation of the Glucose Tolerance Factor and aids in assimilation of insulin.

Gemstones During the Zodiacal Ages

Every 2,160 years, the first point of Aries moves into another zodiacal constellation and thus ushers in a new period of culture and development. Throughout history, different gemstone associations symbolize each of these historical times.

Hindu culture—moonstone

The first point of Aries was in Cancer from 8640–6480 B.C. This was the time of the Hindu culture that emphasized the Moon and imagination and produced splendid elaborate temples with figures of gods and goddesses involved in various fertility rites. The moonstone was important to this culture as symbolic of the Moon's energy.

Persian culture—turquoise

The first point of Aries was in Gemini from 6480–4320 B.C. The Persian culture developed during this time with the doctrine of Zoroasterianism and its emphasis on the duality of good and evil. The turquoise was a sacred stone in this culture for its intermingling of the two colors blue and green.

Egyptian culture—malachite

The first point of Aries was in the sign of Taurus the Bull from 4320–2160 B.C. In Egypt, the sacred bull Apis was worshipped. A bull was chosen and cared for in the temple until it was full grown and then transported in a golden barge over the Nile to the temple of Memphis. Taurus is ruled by the planet Venus whose metal is copper. Malachite contains a lot of copper. Egyptian ladies carried a small tray of malachite with which they painted their eyelids and their hair. Malachite was also mixed with the excrement of cat or cow for use as an eye ointment since eye diseases were prevalent in this culture.

Graeco-Roman culture—agate
The first point of Aries was in Aries from 2160–0 C.E., which corresponds to the height of the Graeco-Roman culture. The Egyptians began to pay homage to the Ram god Ammon. Israelites brought offerings of rams, and in Greece, battles between the city states gave rise to war heroes and a particular Aries mentality. Rome conquered Greece, absorbed its culture, and subjugated a large part of Europe and North Africa. The image of Mars was glorified in the temples, and soldiers wore talismans of agate and sardonyx with this likeness.

Christian culture—amethyst
The Aries point entered Pisces in 0 C.E. and remains there until 2160 C.E. The culture symbolized by the Fishes, the Christian culture, renounced all earthly things and upheld things of the spirit. The Christian converts in Rome inscribed the sign of the fishes on the catacombs. Amethyst, with its purifying quality, was chosen as the gem of this culture. Amethyst was used for meditation and gaining spiritual insights. In the sixteenth century, it was as costly as a diamond (before the discovery of amethyst mines in South America).

Aquarian Age—rose quartz
The Aries point enters Aquarius in 2160 C.E., but we have already been experiencing the beginning of this "new age". The emphasis has been on the individual, on humanitarian projects, and on bringing back ancient forms of the healing arts such as crystals and gems. Rose quartz is a stone associated with the heart chakra; it works on emotional balance and opening up to deeper levels of love and compassion.

The High Priest's Breastplate
Throughout history, perhaps the strongest use of gems for their healing properties was in the breastplate of the high priest. Scholarly texts list several versions of the collections of stones found in the breastplate. Part of the confusion is that there were two breastplates, the Mosaic breastplate and the breastplate of the Second Temple, which was in existence eight centuries later. The twelve stones corresponded to the twelve tribes of Israel and the twelve zodiacal signs.

The Breastplate of Aaron (Mosaic breastplate) gives the following gems:

1. Red jasper

2. Light green serpentine

3. Green feldspar

4. Almandine garnet

5. Lapis lazuli

6. Onyx

7. Brown agate

8. Banded agate

9. Amethyst

10. Yellow jasper

11. Malachite

12. Green jasper or jade

Breastplate of the Second Temple:

1. Carnelian

2. Peridot

3. Emerald

4. Ruby

5. Lapis lazuli

6. Onyx

7. Sapphire or jacinth

8. Banded agate

9. Amethyst

10. Topaz

11. Beryl

12. Green jasper or jade

These stones of the high priest's breastplate are also described in the book of Revelation as the foundation stones of the New Jerusalem. Once again, there is a different list of stones, which may arise from the Hebrew translation.

In one case, when an offender was brought before the high priest for stealing a golden image from a heathen temple in Jericho, the breastplate revealed his guilt, as the stones lost their light and grew dim when his name was pronounced. Other such stories have been attributed to the breastplate.

Planets and Gems

Gemstones correlate to planetary energies and are used in healing conditions characteristic of planetary imbalances. To capture the pure energy of a planet in a crystal, hold the crystal outdoors pointed to that planet in the sky. Ask that the crystal be impregnated with that planet's qualities.

Gems and crystals ruled by each planet are used to strengthen the energy of that planet when it's weak or is being blocked in the natal horoscope, or when it's involved in progressions or transits. As an example, Mars in Cancer might be a weak position for Mars unless it is angular in the horoscope; a Mars gem or crystal could help to strengthen qualities of assertiveness, aggression, and courage along with more physical vitality. Mars could also be receiving a hard aspect from Saturn, natally or by transit, which would also indicate the use of a Mars gemstone since its energies are being blocked or inhibited by Saturn. Another example might be a hard aspect between Venus and Neptune where the individual is trying to express love and compassion, but may not always be clear in the way of displaying it. Gemstones ruled by both Venus and Neptune would be appropriate to use. These stones may be worn in the form of jewelry, kept in a pouch either on one's person or close by, placed under one's pillow at night, or set on one's meditation table. The closer they are to the physical body and to any parts of the body that particularly need the energy, the stronger their effect will be felt.

SUN
Stones ruled by the Sun increase solar energy and vitality. They tend to be warming and beneficial to the circulation. They help to put one in touch with inner power.

Citrine quartz is energizing, lifegiving, and warming. Citrine clusters break up constriction of the navel and third chakra area. They are helpful for poor digestion and constipation, as well as kidney and bladder infections.

Topaz was a symbol of the ancient Egyptian Sun god, a giver of life and fertility and a source of strength to his people. Topaz protects against depression and insomnia; aids circulation of the blood; and prevents and cures hemorrhages, varicose veins, and hemorrhoids. Some golden topaz contains a certain amount of phosphorus as an impurity; it phosphoresces in the dark and waxes and wanes in power with the Moon.

Jasper has different colors: red, brown, yellow, green, or gray; it is worn in the navel for stomachaches. Sometimes it is worn as an amulet in the form of a serpent emitting rays, indicating that the stone itself emits life force. It is recommended for wasting diseases and improves the sense of smell. In Iran, powdered jasper along with turquoise is given for diseases of the gallbladder, liver, and kidneys. Jasper is the last stone mentioned in the high priest's breastplate, and in the New Testament, the first stone mentioned.

Amber is not a stone but the petrified resin of conifers that once grew in forests along the Baltic Sea. When amber is rubbed, it becomes charged with negative electricity. (The Greek word *electron* means "amber.") It is used for asthma, bronchitis, rheumatism, toothache, and heart weakness. According to Greek myth, the tears wept by Phaeton's sisters after his death were turned to amber. (Phaeton was the son of the Sun god who allowed himself to be diverted from the midpath through the heavens while driving the chariot of the Sun. The meaning of the myth is that the individual who squanders the creative force from the Sun in material pleasure will die spiritually, but those things that are charged with solar power can still help the soul.) Amber is a golden gift from the Sun, though it has lain at the bottom of the sea for many years.

Rhodochrosite is raspberry red striped with white, which gives it a peach tone. Thus, it's a combination of orange and pink, the colors of the navel and heart chakras. It has often been called Inca rose because of the location of its main deposits. (It formed as stalagmites in the silver mines of the Incas.) It is used in breaking up blocks in the solar plexus, which are often the result of emotional trauma. These blocks lead to constriction of the diaphragm and a loss of vital force in the body. The energy blockage may result in breathing and lung problems, constipation, digestive disorders, and stomach ulcers. Rhodochrosite is effective in both the emotional body and the physical body for healing.

MOON

Stones ruled by the Moon are used to increase one's sensitivity and intuitive abilities, as well as to aid creative expression.

Moonstone absorbs the healing power of the Moon and acts as a reflection of the wearer. It helps a person to see clearly and protects one while traveling. If a moonstone is hung on the branches of a blossoming fruit tree when the Moon is increasing in light, it is believed the crop will be plentiful. Arab women stitch it into their clothing so that they will be blessed with children. In India it is known as a sacred stone and dream stone. It is said that the best specimens are washed up by the river when the Sun and Moon are in good aspect, and the finest of all appear once in 21 years.

Opal varies in color from milky white to greenish yellow and red. It is translucent and has a glossy sheen. It holds a large amount of water and also some air. In dry air it loses moisture and some of its color, but in damp air these are regained. Opals are said to be seductive and stimulate the erotic nature.

MERCURY

Mercury stones strengthen mental clarity and help to ground the mental energy.

Agate is opaque and patterned and occurs in many forms. Its colors range through reddish brown, orange, and yellow to ochre, gray, and brown. Orpheus took an agate with him during his descent to Hades to strengthen his heart and give him courage. Agate is known to sharpen the sight, illuminate the mind, and bestow eloquence. Powdered, it was mixed in apple juice as a remedy against insanity. In the Gold Coast, agate amulets were worn to prevent snakebite, paralysis, and mental illness. In Greece and Rome, agate amulets were engraved with a dog's head and a lion to protect one from epilepsy and the plague.

Tiger's-eye ranges from the golden yellows associated with Mercury to earthy dark browns. Thus, it has the ability to help ground the mental energies. The eye of the tiger can see through various illusions on the physical plane and understand the higher workings of the mind. Tiger's-eye is also associated with the Sun and the solar plexus due to its deep gold color. It is helpful for those who lack will and appear spaced out in grounding and rooting their energies to their central being.

VENUS

Venus stones work on opening up the heart chakra, expressing love, and manifesting creative energy. They also assist with bringing in the feminine energy and mitigating many female complaints.

Malachite is the ore of copper, which was used in Egypt for many purposes. Cosmetically, it was mixed with water and painted on the eyelids; for healing, it was mixed with cat or cow excrement and placed as a compress on the eyes. It was also used to treat cholera and rheumatism. Copper has a curative effect on diseases like cholera, asthma, cardiac spasm, and also degenerative diseases like cancer.

Tourmaline is green underneath and pink on top, which are the two colors associated with Venus. It was used in the Middle Ages as a meditation stone. The Rosicrucians and alchemists called tourmaline *christus stone*, symbolizing the ascent of matter (green Earth) to sublime love (rose pink). Tourmaline attracts abundance and prosperity toward the wearer; it inspires creativity and strengthens the ability to project, create, and manifest goals.

Emerald is a stone of Libra that was supposed to stabilize the marriage bond. If there was any unfaithfulness, it became dull. In Egypt, women wore emeralds engraved with a picture of Isis, the Universal Mother. They were the guardians of spring and symbolized the process of generation and ripening. Emeralds keep the wearer fresh and youthful and strengthen the sight.

Green aventurine is a quartz with a pure green ray. It is good for dissolving emotions that are causing constrictions in the heart area and may be used in conjunction with malachite, which brings emotions to the surface. It is also a stone that is a master healer in that it can bring the green healing ray into any part of the body that is diseased or imbalanced. Green aventurine can be carried or worn in times of particular stress since it will affect all areas of the being.

Rose quartz is a healing stone for the heart chakra. The pink color comforts and heals any wounds the heart has accumulated. Rose quartz initiates any expressions of love and is a good stone for those just beginning to open up to their true feelings. It is used in crystal healings, often utilizing three rose quartz crystals, with one over the heart chakra, one above it, and one below it. Amethyst is frequently used along with it to balance the mental energy; it is placed near the third eye.

Kunzite is a stone associated with the heart chakra that works with emotional equilibrium. It is used to help channel love into external expression and to let go of any old fears and sorrows. The crystal contains both pale pink and violet hues, which shows that it can create a balance between the higher mind (third eye center) and the heart. It works with transforming old thought patterns that are associated with emotional blocks. Kunzite has the purest transparency of any stone in the pink spectrum—it symbolizes a state of unconditional love and the pure expression of love.

MARS

Mars gems increase the vitality, strengthen the will, impart aggressiveness and assertiveness, and bring more iron to the blood. To cool down Mars energy, a Venus stone should be used; to structure it, a Saturn stone may prove beneficial.

Bloodstone is deep green with splotches of red and is associated with mysticism in India, where much of it is mined. It is used to staunch hemorrhages and to prevent nosebleeds. It purifies the blood and strengthens the blood purifying organs—the kidneys, liver, and spleen. It directs the healing color of green into the bloodstream, creating a state of detoxification. It can be placed over areas of congestion in the body and used for sluggish circulation. Bloodstone affects the kundalini center and moves the energy up and down the spine. For those who have purified their bodies, it enables the physical vehicle to carry greater amounts of light and energy.

Carnelian is a red-orange agate composed of silicon dioxide or quartz. It does not project and emanate light as the higher vibration transparent stones, but it reflects back the depth of color of the physical world. It grounds energy and can be used for confusion and absent-mindedness. It is helpful for infertility or impotency when placed around the navel and pelvic area. It stimulates the second chakra and clears the reproductive organs of any blockages.

Ruby aids in circulation of the blood and in cleansing it of any infection. It dissolves blood clots, strengthens the adrenal glands, and staunches the flow of blood when ground into a paste with water. It gives initiative and imparts energy, courage, passion, and victory to the wearer. Water in which a ruby had been soaked was used as a means of healing and restoring youth.

Garnet gives a strong will, self-confidence, pride, and success. It is used for clairvoyance and was employed by the ancients to reveal hidden places and to find buried treasures, thus associating it with the sign Scorpio. Garnet was used in healing for skin eruptions. Garnets impart passion along with power, energy, and courage. In Italy, they were worn by widows to attract a new mate.

Hematite is the Dutch bloodstone; it is dark red-gray in color. Engraved pieces of hematite were found in ancient Egyptian tombs and in the mines of Babylon. Soldiers often carry it with them as it strengthens the heart, imparts courage and endurance, and protects from danger. It is good for rapid pulse and bloodshot eyes. Hematite is also found in crystalline form, but it is the nodules embedded in red ironstone that are used in jewelry.

JUPITER

Jupiter stones can be used for many types of healing. Some of them work to cleanse the liver and increase bile flow; some have been used to protect riders and their horses.

Turquoise has always been considered a holy gem. It treats eye problems as well as ailments of an inflammatory or feverish origin. The Egyptians felt the earthy green color joined the heavenly blue color in giving the turquoise its special quality. Turquoise loses color when its wearer is ill or in danger; it turns a dull yellow when worn by a person with liver problems. The stone absorbs harmful vibrations, sometimes shattering. It was a sacred stone in Persia during the time of Zoroaster. In the Orient, turquoise is used to protect riders and their steeds; strings of turquoise beads are attached to the horses' harnesses in order to make them sure-footed on narrow mountain paths. The Arabs wore a turquoise between three pearls on their headbands; at the hour of Jupiter, they took the stone in their right hand and made wishes on it. The Native Americans have always considered turquoise their sacred stone and use it in making jewelry and ritual objects.

Chrysocolla is a semiprecious stone like turquoise, being opaque and dull in luster. Its blue-green color represents the Divine Mother and the virtues of compassion, humility, and patience. It is used for female disorders and can assist in balancing hormones after miscarriages, abortions, and hysterectomies. It is an emotional balancer and can be placed over the heart chakra to bring control. As a cooling stone, it lowers fevers, heals burns, neutralizes anger, and calms the nerves. It is also a stone of Venus and works well on the throat chakra for thyroid imbalance, voice problems, and sore throats.

Some of the stones ruled by the Sun, like topaz, citrine quartz, and jasper, are also ruled by Jupiter since they increase bile flow.

SATURN

Gems of Saturn are often used to help put ideas and projects into form. Some Saturn gems are also used to break up old patterns and treat conditions as arthritis and rheumatism.

Diamond is the hardest of the gems, and it has always been associated with the marriage ceremony. It amplifies the searching and seeking within the soul and the attaining of spiritual clarity. Internally, diamonds strengthen the body, nourish the tissues, and improve the complexion. Diamonds come in different shapes; sometimes they are round and sometimes they are four-sided pyramids. Four is the number of Saturn.

Onyx is a variety of agate; black onyx has been colored artificially for years. It is also called "nagel" stone or "nail" stone as it is good for nails, hair, and skin. It brings seriousness, perseverance, humility, deep thoughts, spiritual strength, reserve, and fearlessness. It is good for circulatory disorders and accidents. Onyx is used in rosaries to aid thought concentration; it is also employed in signet rings and on articles of clothing worn during mourning. The onyx helps hearing and listening; it is given in high homeopathic potencies for certain ear diseases.

Green calcite works with mental balance in the sense of releasing outdated concepts and ushering in new ones. When mental and emotional concepts become very rigid, they often manifest in the bones, ligaments, tendons, and cartilage. Green calcite is helpful in these cases, which often turn into arthritis, rheumatism, and tendonitis. It can help channel healing into bone tissue. It is also good for cooling fiery complaints like fevers and emotional conditions related to anger.

URANUS

Stones ruled by Uranus are used to bring in new ideas and stimulation to the higher mental centers and to help break up old patterns. They are also calming to the nervous system when strong Uranian vibrations are present.

Lapis lazuli is a deep blue stone mixed with white calcite containing flecks of gold or pyrite. It has a strong spiritual vibration and was one of the stones in the high priest's breastplate. Moses inscribed the Ten Commandments on blocks of lapis. In ancient Egypt it was known as the stone of the gods; the gold flecks reflected the stars in the night sky and were regarded as touchstones for truth. The stone was ground and made into dyes that colored the robes of the high priests and those of royal blood. The Egyptians felt that by wearing this color they became representatives of the gods and that supernatural forces would empower their lives. Lapis was also pulverized and used as a remedy for certain maladies and as a contraindicator for poisons.

By pulverizing the stone, lapis was made into a poultice and placed upon the crown of the head. As it dried, it would draw out the demons and cleanse the soul's impurities. In extreme cases, a small hole was drilled in the skull, and the lapis mixture was poured into the head of the possessed. It was soaked in warm water and applied to swellings and painful nerves and used as an eyewash. Lapis is one of seven precious stones in Buddhism. It is used to help cleanse or purge the aura; it is often placed on the third eye area to penetrate subconscious blockages. Lapis represents symbolically going through darkness to find one's deeper self; the gold specks symbolize the wisdom that is achieved.

Sapphire is a sacred stone among the Buddhists. It is believed to be a powerful influence for purity; it is used in ecclesiastical rings in the Catholic church. Ayurvedic physicians in India employ it to treat rheumatism, colic, and mental illness. Sapphire protects the eyes and heart and overcomes melancholy, fever, and effects of poison. Its color changes are a warning that one is about to come into contact with some negative influence. (The stone referred to as sapphire in the Bible is really lapis.)

Aquamarine is a stone of mystics; it is associated with Uranus and gives clarity of mental vision and omniscience. Since it is good for the eyes, glasses used to be made from it. It is best worn in a long necklace so that it can hang down beside the heart and influence the solar plexus. It helps with nerve pains, glandular troubles, disorders of the neck, jaw, and throat, toothaches, as well as liver and eye trouble.

Azurite is a deep indigo blue stone, which was used by the high priests and priestesses in Egypt to raise their consciousness and contact divine energy. Azurite crystals are used to bring healing to parts of the body and to break up old subconscious patterns while gathering new ideas and energy in the mental realm. Azurite can be placed on any part of the body where there is a physical blockage; as the deep blue ray penetrates and breaks up the energy, the emotional and psychic reasons causing the block may become apparent.

NEPTUNE

Gems associated with the planet Neptune work to increase psychic sensitivity, to enhance receptivity to music and poetry, and to work with higher states of consciousness.

Amethyst has always been associated with royalty due to its purple color. It draws to it forces being directed to a particular body and repels vibrations the body does not need. It is used for changes of consciousness from normal waking states into areas of altered awareness. The amethyst ray reflects the ability to transform from one reality to another; therefore, it is one of the best stones for meditation and can be placed over the third eye. It is helpful for those who are grieving and those who are crossing over. Since its color is a combination of red and blue, it brings peace to those who are angry and hot-headed; it is also good for tension resulting from overwork and stress. Amethyst is used for migraines and for nightmares or bad dreams where it is placed under the pillow before going to sleep. Amethyst also protects against drunkenness and poisons; it counteracts the absentmindedness of Neptune and Pisces and gives clarity in prophecy and interpretation of dreams. Amethyst helps fishermen make catches and encourages the growth of plants below the ground. It is used for skin diseases (placed in boiling water, the liquid is used to cleanse the skin) as well as for color blindness. In the Middle Ages, it was more expensive than the diamond, but as people began to take less interest in spiritual matters, its value lessened. The discovery of rich amethyst mines in South America also changed its value.

Fluorite comes in clusters, octahedrons, and pyramids. It enables the mind to maintain a meditative state while in the midst of physical activity. It represents the polarity of amethyst, which is the internal experience of surrendering the mind. Fluorite brings that experience into daily thought processes, allowing one to see the wisdom behind the appearances in the outer world. It brings onto the physical plane higher forms of truth. Fluorite can be used in treating certain types of mental illness and disturbances in brain wave frequencies. It increases the electrical charge of the brain cells, which brings more life force into the brain and thus helps to expand consciousness.

Jade is also ruled by Venus due to its green color. It is considered the most precious stone in China and Japan; the Chinese believe it provides a link between the spiritual and the worldly. The ancient Egyptians used it in amulets and believed it to have mystical powers. Jade is a good meditation stone; it may be kept in the pocket and rubbed. It rivals nephrite in being one of the strongest of stones that can withstand greater pressure than steel. In antiquity, spear points, axe heads, and knives were made from it. In ancient Mexico, the Mayans cut whole scenes out of jade; many of these have been excavated at the site of ancient temples. The Conquistadores saw the Mexicans using jade and nephrite as remedies for the kidneys. Jade is said to prolong life, help in childbirth, protect from accidents, and provide a large family. In China imperial jade is emerald green in color, shining, and perfect. The last Empress of China had 3,000 ivory cabinets full of this stone.

Sugilite (also known as luvulite) has a deep purple color, much deeper than amethyst or fluorite, suggesting that it really helps in grounding the energy from the third eye or sixth chakra. It is an excellent stone to be used by supersensitive souls who tend to take in the vibrations of others and negative planetary energies. It is a good stone for meditation or rituals and can be cleansing to the lymph system if placed on the groin or near the lymph glands. There is not much sugilite on the planet at this particular time, but perhaps more will be available as we become prepared to use it.

Coral is also ruled by Mars due to its red color. Coral takes the form of reefs growing on the floor of warm seas in Polynesia, off the coast of Japan, and in the Mediterranean. Red coral is often made into jewelry. If the coral becomes pale, the wearer is said to be anemic and weak. Coral is used as a tonic for the blood, a heart stimulant, and a remedy against melancholy. It raises a person's vibrations and increases receptivity to creative forces.

PLUTO

Gemstones associated with Pluto help to transform old energy patterns and release emotional states.

Smoky quartz contains the highest amount of light force in a dark stone. It is capable of helping to channel energy from the crown chakra into the first chakra and ground it on the physical plane. It also aids in bringing the energy from the heart chakra into the root chakra. It is good for those who are depressed, fatigued, uncertain about their role in the world, or suicidal. Smoky quartz helps to dissolve toxins in the body associated with the excretory system. Thus, it works on cleansing physically as well as psychically.

Black obsidian draws higher forces into the body to be used in a physically active way. It also acts as a mirror to reflect certain flaws in one's nature and magnify fears, insecurities, and egocentric attitudes. It brings these "dark areas" into the light. In this sense, it represents all the higher energies associated with the color black. As one of the highest colors worn by advanced initiates of the mystery schools, black symbolizes mastery over the physical plane. (In the martial arts, the "black belt" is the ultimate achievement and represents the ability to ground the "chi" energy.) Black obsidian balls are powerful meditation pieces. In crystal healings, black obsidian stones are placed upon the groin or on the navel to ground higher energies into the body.

Jet is very soft and easily worked into jewelry. Jet amulets were used to dispel depression and fear and to protect from thunderstorms. In powdered form, jet was mixed with beeswax and made into an ointment to treat tumors; it was also mixed with water and used for toothaches. The powder was burned to produce fumes, which were used to repel germs of plagues and as a fumigant. The fumes were also used to treat epilepsy and combat hysteria.

Pearl is a Pluto gem in the sense that it is created by the irritation of an organism that defends itself by secreting self-protecting material. Thus, the formation of beauty occurs by the overcoming of hardship. Pearls have been used to increase fertility. They have been discovered in old Toltec and Aztec graves and in Egyptian mummy cases. In the Orient, a tincture made from pearl is drunk during the mourning period.

Flower Remedies and Astrological Signs

Flower essences are a part of the new medicine of vibrational healing, which seeks to balance the subtle bodies in an effort to prevent any latent energetic conditions from manifesting on the physical plane. If the higher mental and emotional vehicles are in balance, then the factors on the causative plane that create physical imbalance or disease need not have a physical effect.

Flower remedies are a distillation of the essences of certain flowers in a solution of water and a small amount of alcohol, which acts as a preservative. The petals of the flowers are gathered, placed in water, and infused with sunlight, enabling the liquid to resonate with the "aura," or quintessence, of the flower. This liquid is then preserved with alcohol and used as the "mother liquid" from which stock bottles are made. They may be taken internally through the mouth in a dropper or placed in a bath, where they can penetrate the entire body. Often, more than one essence is used since certain essences work well together in balancing various emotional states.

Flower essences contain the etheric energy of the plant and first penetrate the circulatory system, then the nervous system. They often work better on those whose physical vehicles are cleansed through fasting and purer diets. For individuals who have attained balanced physical and emotional vehicles, certain combinations of flower essences may be substituted for vitamin and mineral supplements. This is because once the imbalances in the higher bodies are eliminated, there is a more balanced state physically. We know that many sensitive souls can acquire their nutrients by breathing pure air and eating a diet of simple pure foods. As we each evolve, we need fewer nutrients on a gross physical level, but more on an etheric level. This transmutation of the subtle essences to feed the physical body was part of the ancient science of alchemy.

There are several different ways of determining which essences are best for each individual at a particular time period. Most important is the interview and consultation done by the practitioner. The initial interview should include a complete health history of the client—both physical and emotional. The client should be queried on diet, medications, vitamin and mineral supplements, and any other treatments the person is undergoing, as well as on any life situations that may be creating stress.

Utilizing the astrological horoscope is extremely helpful in assessing personality traits. Progressions and transits indicate the cycles one is undergoing and reveal possible imbalances, emotionally and physically, during these time periods. Since the flower essences deal with emotional states, it is possible to correlate the various emotions with the signs and planets and make a list of these after analyzing the horoscope.

Basic Emotions as Seen in the Horoscope

Anxiety and worry—Look at Mercury and Uranus. Are there a lot of hard aspects to these planets? How prominent are the signs Gemini and Virgo in the horoscope? Are there many planets in these signs? How are they aspected?

Fears—Examine Saturn and Pluto and their aspects. Saturn's sign often gives a key to the area of one's fears. Several people with Saturn in Scorpio, for example, have a fear of drowning and do not swim because of this. There may be many causes of this, including childhood traumas and past life incidents, but they still retain the fear.

Love and the capacity to express it—Look at Venus, Venus-Mars aspects, Venus-Saturn aspects, and Venus-Pluto aspects. Often, one with hard aspects from Venus to Saturn or Mars has difficulty expressing his or her emotions and feelings; with the hard aspects to Pluto, one is called upon to transform these feelings into other modes of expression.

Anger—Check out Mars: its sign, house, and aspects. Mars in the twelfth house has difficulty expressing anger; so does Mars in Cancer and Mars in

Pisces. With hard aspects from Saturn, Mars tends to hold back as well. With hard aspects to Pluto, there may be explosions and a violent temper.

Jealousy—Examine the aspects to a Scorpio Sun, Moon, Venus, and Ascendant. With hard aspects from the Moon to Mars or Pluto or from Venus to Mars or Pluto, there may be a tendency to jealousy.

Detached—Often, several planets in Aquarius, an Aquarius Moon (especially if it's aspected to Saturn) or Aquarius rising may make one appear aloof or detached emotionally.

Overly sensitive—Predominant water in the horoscope, an angular Moon or Neptune, and hard aspects between the Moon and Neptune cause one to be hypersensitive to others and to the environment.

"Spaced out" or ungrounded—A strong Pisces emphasis or twelfth house planets, as well as hard aspects from Neptune to the Moon or Ascendant, may make one appear "spacy" or ungrounded.

Holding on to old patterns—Lots of fixed signs, several planets in Capricorn, or Saturn elevated may cause one to become crystallized and hold on to old emotional behavior.

Additional methods of choosing flower essences include radiesthesia (the use of the pendulum), which works with quantum vibrations, and applied kinesiology, or muscle testing. When the pendulum is used, the remedies may be tested in the kit or by having the client hold them. With muscle testing, the client holds each remedy to see which ones will be strengthening. It is important to test combinations of remedies in these ways as well, since they can have a synergistic effect.

There are several different kinds of flower remedies available. The most well-known are the Bach Flower Remedies developed by Dr. Edward Bach, an English physician who was the first to reveal how the essences of wildflowers and plants could be utilized in healing. Dr. Bach roamed the English countryside observing the various flowers—their colors, aromas, where they grew, and when they blossomed—and sensing their life force. He then experimented with many of these and saw that by distilling the essences of these flowers and administering them to his patients, various emotional states could be balanced thereby preventing disease in the physical body. Dr. Bach composed a repertory of 38 flower essences, which are used individually or in combination.

In the United States, pioneering work with flower remedies was begun by Richard Katz, a practitioner trained in various forms of healing, in the 1970s.

Mr. Katz found growing in the mountains of Northern California many plants and flowers that proved extremely healing. He later expanded his research throughout the world; many essences of the Flower Essence Society (FES), which he founded with his wife Patricia Kaminski, have been developed in Hawaii, Australia, and several European countries where the two have traveled. At present, several FES kits plus a research kit are available.

Other popular flower essence kits include the Perelandra essences developed by Machaelle Small-Wright on her land in Virginia. She has a book, *Flower Essences* (Perelandra, Ltd., 1988), which discusses her rose and vegetable essences.

In this chapter, I chose to include those essences with which I have the greatest familiarity. These include the Bach Repertory and many of the essences developed by the FES.

I have attempted to categorize the essences through the twelve signs of the zodiac since each sign represents an archetypal energy pattern. Under each sign, I list essences that help to counteract the particular qualities mentioned, as well as those that stimulate these qualities. For example, under the sign Aries, impatiens helps to calm down any fiery, hotheaded qualities, while Indian paintbrush or cayenne stimulates the vital and fiery energies. With each essence, certain aspect patterns and transits are mentioned to aid the astrologer in selecting individual remedies. Transits refer to the hard aspects only.

ARIES

Arians tends to be impatient, impulsive, headstrong, ego-centered, and often selfish. They need to learn to be aware of the needs of others and also to follow through and complete projects. On a positive note, Arians are independent, excel at starting new projects, and have an abundance of creative vital energy.

Bach Remedies

Impatiens helps to bring about a slow, patient quality, relieve muscular tension often accompanying the mental tension, and catalyze a feeling of gentleness and sympathy toward others. It is good for those who have Mercury-Mars hard aspects, Mars-Saturn hard aspects, and Saturn in Aries.

Heather deals with the self-centeredness and self-concern of the Aries personality. It works to develop the qualities of understanding and selflessness and a willingness to help others. It is suggested for those who have several planets in Aries or with Aries in the first house.

Vine is a remedy that is helpful for those personalities who tend to dominate; it brings out compassionate feelings and tones down aggressive qualities. This remedy works well for conjunctions between Mars and the Sun, or an angular Mars.

FES Remedies

Scarlet monkeyflower deals with emotional fears, which are very Martian in their nature. It helps people who repress anger and aggression. It is also beneficial for those who lack a certain vitality or Mars energy, which may be connected with their holding back of strong emotions. This is a good remedy for those who have hard aspects between Mars and Saturn or Neptune, or hard aspects between Mars and Pluto.

Indian paintbrush has a brilliant red color found on the red-tipped leaves close to the flowers. Since the color penetrates into the leafy region, it acts as an awakener and vitalizer. The essence thus helps one to connect creativity and artistic expression with the vital life force. It works to overcome frustration and creative stagnation and can also be used to enhance vitality. Indian paintbrush is a good remedy for those who have hard aspects between the Sun and Mars or Saturn or hard aspects between Mars and Saturn or Neptune.

Trumpet vine is shaped like a trumpet with red-orange flowers. It allows a certain vitality and force to come through in communications and is thus helpful to those who need to bring more emotional force into their speech. It is beneficial for those who have Moon-Saturn and Mercury-Saturn hard aspects, and combinations of Mars/Saturn/Moon, Mars/Saturn/Mercury, and Venus/Saturn/Mars aspects.

Cayenne works as an herb to stimulate circulation in the physical body. As a flower essence, it acts as a catalyst to move one who is apathetic, phlegmatic, or stuck in a negative situation. It is used to fire the will and aids those with hard aspects between Mars and Saturn, Neptune, the Sun, or between Saturn and the Sun.

Tiger lily transmutes hostility and aggressiveness into positive action for the good of others. It is a remedy often used by businessmen to mellow out their energy in the competitive world. It is also used by many women in transitional states such as menopause, to help balance female energy. Lily is a flower related to the feminine. Homeopathically, it is used to heal the female organs. Tiger lily is a helpful remedy for those with hard aspects between the Moon and Mars or between planets in Aries and Cancer.

TAURUS

Taureans tend to be fixed in their emotional patterns, holding on to possessions and getting rooted too deeply in material concerns. Taureans can often be sluggish and have problems with their metabolism. The Venusian influence can make them overly indulgent as well. When balanced, a Taurus is warm, loving, sensual, has strong artistic capabilities, works well with plants and Earth energy, and is adept at handling practical issues.

Bach Remedies

Chestnut bud is for those who get stuck in the same patterns and often need to repeat the same lesson many times. They do not seem to learn from their experience or let go of the past. This is a helpful remedy for those with several planets in Taurus, and for strong Saturn types.

Chicory is helpful for unblocking the emotions, for becoming nonpossessive of others, and for allowing a free flow of selfless love. It may be indicated for those who have Venus-Saturn or Venus-Mars hard aspects.

FES Remedies

Iris is a truly Venusian flower named for the Greek goddess of the rainbow that symbolizes the love that flows from Heaven to Earth. Iris can aid in expressing blocked creative energies and in manifesting the higher or divine nature of love. It is useful for those with hard aspects between Venus and Neptune or Pluto.

Bleeding heart has heart-shaped flowers and deals with the emotional pain of "brokenheartedness." It encourages emotional clarity and self-control. It can be used at the death or separation of a loved one, or in a relationship where personal feelings have created a restriction and more detachment is needed. It is a remedy often called for during Uranus transits of the Moon and Venus.

California wild rose, like other roses, has been associated with the heart and the planet Venus. The rose has beautiful colored flowers and a wonderful fragrance, but also thorns, symbolizing the process of transmutation necessary to experience the deepest levels of love. The rose is shaped like the heart and duplicates its process of contraction and expansion. (The rosebud makes a sharp contraction before blossoming.) As an essence, the California wild rose helps those who need to take hold of life more strongly and to develop enthusiasm and caring, working through their indifference, apathy, and escapism.

It is a soothing essence and may be used as a balm for the heart. It is often called for by those who have hard aspects between Venus and Saturn and between the Moon and Saturn.

Tansy blooms for quite a while, and its name derives from the Greek *athanaton*, which means "immortal." It induces those who tend to be sluggish and need to overcome their inertia to move forward in their particular process. This may be a helpful remedy for those with the Moon in Taurus or several planets in Taurus.

Hound's tongue is a stout plant that is often used for weight loss. Those for whom this remedy is helpful have bodies that tend to be overly earthbound. Those with a Taurus Ascendant, Sun or Moon or several planets in Taurus may find this essence useful.

GEMINI

Geminis can scatter their energies, become involved in too many projects, and get overly mental. Gemini natives need to focus and ground their energies. The positive vibration of Gemini is the utilization of their diverse talents, their ability to write, speak, and teach, and to explore their roles as communicators and networkers.

Bach Remedies

White chestnut helps in attaining a calm, clear, quiet mind without the constant clutter of unwanted thoughts. This may be called for with Mercury in one of the mutable signs or with hard aspects between Mercury and Uranus, Mars, the Moon, or Jupiter.

Hornbeam works to combat mental and physical exhaustion that results from the mind dwelling on its own problems for too long. This remedy is useful for those who have several planets in Gemini or hard aspects between Mercury and the Moon or Mars.

Mimulus works with anxieties, fears, and doubts of known origins. It helps one to understand and deal with trials in life and to develop courage and equanimity in the face of any difficulties. Mimulus aids those with hard aspects from Pluto or Neptune to Mercury.

FES Remedies

Morning glory is helpful in balancing the nervous system. It is good for restlessness, hyperactivity, and nervous habits. It has also been useful for insomnia. Morning glory works well with Mercury-Uranus hard aspects, Mars-Uranus hard aspects, Jupiter-Uranus hard aspects, an angular Uranus, and Uranus transits in general.

Madia is a good flower essence for centering and focusing. It is useful for those who are easily distracted and for those who need specific focus when working on important projects. Madia may be recommended for Mercury-Saturn and Mercury-Jupiter hard aspects.

Shasta daisy is a member of the composite/sunflower family along with madia, and thus works with the principle of integration and synthesis. It assists in combining information from many diverse sources and focusing on a particular path. This is a helpful remedy during Saturn transits to Mercury and also during Uranus transits to Mercury.

Blackberry enables us to become more aware of our thought processes, helping us to direct these thoughts so they won't be like the tangled mess of the blackberry plant, but more focused and discriminating. It helps to clear up mental confusion and works as a bridge from the more abstract mental levels to the more concrete. Blackberry is good for hard aspects between Mercury and Neptune, Mercury and Uranus, and sometimes Mercury and Jupiter. It is also good for those who have several planets in Gemini or Sagittarius.

Rabbitbrush essence aids those dealing with complex situations who need to develop alertness and sharp awareness to see all the details. It also works on integrating details into the total picture. It is called for during Uranus and Neptune transits to Mercury.

Lavender essence helps to balance the nervous system in certain sensitive and high-strung individuals. They often have difficulties in making a transition between thoughts of the spiritual world and those of the more physical earthy reality. It is a good remedy for those having hard aspects between Mercury and Uranus or Neptune. It is also helpful during transits of Uranus and Neptune to Mercury.

Yerba santa as an herbal remedy is useful in counteracting watery conditions like mucus and bronchial congestion. It brings a drying quality and allows the air to move through the lungs. The flower essence soothes emotional trauma, providing a release of internal pain; it is useful for melancholy and where there is a tendency for the chest to droop, signifying depression. It may be helpful for Mercury-Saturn and Mercury-Pluto hard aspects.

CANCER

Cancers tend to be self-protective, hiding inside their shell, clinging to the past and old emotional attachments, and overly sensitive. When balanced, a Cancer is warm, nurturing, loving, and sensitive to the needs of others.

Bach Remedies

Chicory works with letting go of old emotions and promoting selfless, compassionate feelings. It is good for Moon-Saturn, Moon-Pluto, Venus-Saturn, and Venus-Pluto hard aspects.

Honeysuckle counteracts nostalgia, living in the past, and holding on to past feelings and emotions. Honeysuckle may be indicated in hard aspects between the Moon and Saturn or Pluto.

Larch is a pine tree indigenous to Central Europe. It is a very hardy tree and is used as a "nurse" for less sturdy growing trees. The larch remedy is good for lack of confidence and anticipation of failure. When balanced, one is willing to take risks and not be discouraged by the results. This is a good remedy for hard aspects between the Moon and Saturn as well as for transits of Saturn to the Moon.

Centaury is a helpful remedy for those who are too easily influenced by the will of others. These people need to learn to stand up for themselves and be more independent and adventuresome. Their vitality can also be easily drained. When balanced, the qualities of service are present without a loss of individuality. Strong Cancerian individuals and those with angular Moons, as well as those with hard aspects from the Moon to Neptune, often find this remedy helpful.

Red chestnut is used for fears and anxieties that one has for others who are ill and those with whom one spends time. This remedy enables an individual to send out thoughts of health and well-being to others and remain calm and centered in any emergency. Red chestnut may be helpful to those who have hard aspects between the Moon and Mercury and those with combinations of Moon/Mercury/Pluto or Moon/Mercury/Mars aspects.

FES Remedies

Chamomile is helpful at times of emotional unrest and anxiety. (German chamomile is called *Matricaria chamomilla*, which means "mothering.") It is a nurturing essence that brings a more objective view of the emotions during periods of stress. It is a good remedy for children, especially when they have digestive problems. Chamomile may be used for Uranus-Moon hard aspects, Mars-Moon hard aspects, and transits of Uranus to the Moon.

Buttercup is a good remedy for those who are shy or withdrawn and need to be encouraged to share their light with others. Just as the small buttercup sheds its light among the other flowers, so the person who is bringing up small children or taking care of a garden is shedding light among others and needs to be reminded of the importance of this. Buttercup may be called for by those with a strong Cancer influence in their horoscope, with an angular Moon, or with Moon-Saturn or Moon-Sun hard aspects.

Golden eardrops deals with childhood memories and early patterns of emotional experience. Old memories are often stirred up with this essence and brought to awareness; thus it has been called "Golden Yeardrops." Releasing tears is often helpful in balancing the heart center. It is a good remedy for transits of Saturn, Uranus, Neptune, and Pluto to the Moon.

Pomegranate has had special significance throughout history as a symbol of love and maternal nurturing. It is used as a feminine symbol in the Tarot card of the High Priestess. The pomegranate essence works with the feminine creative drive and its integration in the outside world. It is helpful for women dealing with problems of balancing motherhood and career. Pomegranate brings out a maternal nurturing quality. It is a good remedy for those with Moon-Saturn or Moon-Sun hard aspects as well as with Capricorn and Virgo Moons.

Mariposa lily grows in rocky, mountainous terrain, yet has the quality of soft nurturance. It is of benefit for those who have suffered trauma in parent-child bonding and for those who have felt unloved and uncared for. It makes one receptive to love and heals feelings of alienation. It is a good remedy for children. Those with hard aspects between the Moon and Saturn or the Sun as well as those with Capricorn Moons often require this remedy.

Pink yarrow is a useful remedy for those who take in the emotions of others. See Pisces and the discussion of yarrow.

LEO

Leos can be proud, boastful, dominating, inflexible, ambitious, and filled with their own ego needs. The positive traits of Leo are courage, strong leadership abilities, and a warm, open heart.

Bach Remedies

Vine helps to bring out the true leadership qualities of Leo in a positive manner. Rather than dominating, one with strong Leo aspects can become the wise, understanding, and compassionate ruler or teacher. This remedy works well for hard aspects between Mars and the Sun, for an angular Mars, and for hard aspects between Mars and Pluto, especially a Mars-Pluto conjunction in Leo.

FES Remedies

Borage brings humor and lightness as well as a calm, quiet courage to those who use it. As an herb, borage is high in magnesium, which is associated with the heart and with Leo. It is an uplifting flower, making one happy in heart. Borage is helpful with hard aspects from Saturn or Pluto to the Sun and combinations of Sun/Saturn/Pluto, Mars/Saturn/ Pluto, and Mars/Saturn/Sun.

Sunflower turns its head toward the Sun, following the Sun's path across the sky. To the ancient Aztecs and Incas, the sunflower represented the earthly symbol of the Sun's energy; priests and priestesses wore representations of the sunflower during ceremonies of Sun worship. The essence of this flower helps balance ego with spirituality, helping to harmonize the ego with the higher self. It also deals with raising the kundalini energy, which travels up the spine and activates the other chakric centers. This is a very good remedy for transits of Pluto or Neptune to the Sun and of Pluto to Mars or Neptune. The sunflower blooms during the month of Leo.

Nasturtium is another flower whose hue is the bright golden light of the Sun. It is good for enhancing vital energy and has been used as an ingredient in massage oils. It is also a good balance for those who are overly intellectual and spend much of their time indoors. Nasturtium may be helpful for those with Sun-Saturn or Sun-Mars hard aspects, as well as for those with an air sign emphasis.

Dandelion ("tooth of the lion") essence works on the relationship of the physical body to cosmic energy. When there is a lot of tension in the physical body, there is a similar constriction and inflexibility in the emotional and etheric bodies. If dandelion is used with bodywork, added to massage oils, or applied to the skin directly, it works on the musculature of the body. Dandelion is a helpful essence for those with several planets in Leo, with Saturn in Leo, or with Saturn conjunct the Sun, Moon, or Ascendant.

VIRGO

Virgos tend to be overly critical, seeking perfection in themselves and others, and are often too attached to purification and cleanliness. The positive qualities of Virgo manifest in service to others, a fine discriminating intellect, and a good grasp of earthy, practical needs.

Bach Remedies

Beech helps balance the intolerant, critical quality of Virgo. It brings out the forgiving, compassionate aspects of selfless service. Beech is often helpful for those who have several planets in Virgo or Saturn in Virgo.

Crab apple is cleansing to both body and mind. It helps to clear the mind of trivial thoughts and to purify the body of all external blemishes and conditions. It also enables one to see the inner chaos present behind physical disorders. Crab apple is useful for Pluto transits, especially to the Ascendant, Sun, Moon, Venus, Mars, and Saturn.

Pine aids those who suffer from self-reproach and guilt. It helps them to take on responsibilities and to be aware of their own capabilities while at the same time possessing a genuine humility. Pine is sometimes called for by those who have Saturn in Virgo or Pisces as well as those with several planets in Virgo or Pisces.

FES Remedies

Dill helps in assimilating experiences and in digesting psychic and mental influences. It balances us when we are overloaded or overstimulated from too much input. On the physical level, dill is used for digestive complaints; dill leaf and seed expel flatulence (Virgo rules the intestines). Dill remedy is often called for with a strongly elevated Mercury or Uranus having hard aspects to the Moon or Mars.

Corn is known as *Zea mays*. The genus *Zea* is one of the 20 members of the grass family and derives from the Greek word for "grain" or "cereal." The species *mays* comes from a Native American word *maiz* meaning "Universal Mother." Corn represents the bounty of the Earth Mother and the benevolence of the Great Spirit. It therefore invokes the relationship between Heaven and Earth as well as that of human beings to each other. The corn essence helps to find one's balance with Earth/Heaven or the social axis in relation to one's inner psychic balance. Corn helps to bring out the nurturing, serving, mothering aspect. It is useful for those with a strong Virgo influence, with many planets in the sixth house, Saturn in Virgo, or Saturn in Cancer.

Filaree is for those who tend to get caught up in petty worries, who need to gain perspective on their larger destiny and let go of their troubles. This is a helpful remedy for those with several planets in Virgo or Gemini and hard aspects from the Moon to Mercury.

LIBRA

Librans can be indecisive, place too much energy into relationships, and not pay as much attention to individual needs. The positive qualities of Libra are a balance between relationships and time spent alone, a loving peaceful nature, and a confident display of creative talent.

Bach Remedies

Scleranthus aids those who are uncertain of their plans, experience extremes of emotion, and waste time trying to make decisions. It helps them to be poised, calm, determined, and quick in their actions. Scleranthus is useful for those who have their Moon in hard aspect to Neptune or Mercury, several planets in Libra, Gemini, or Pisces, or a strong mutable emphasis in their horoscope.

Agrimony allows one to experience a deep inner self-acceptance to match outward conviviality and to seek companionship, not as an escape but as a true sharing of inner peace. Agrimony may be called for by those who have Saturn in Libra or Venus-Saturn hard aspects.

Cerato helps those who doubt their own abilities; they tend to follow the advice of others even when it doesn't agree with their own intuitions. This essence strengthens the ability to judge for oneself and follow one's own guidance. Cerato is often used by those with hard aspects between the Moon and Saturn or Neptune or with several planets in Pisces or the twelfth house.

FES Remedies

Sweet pea works in harmonizing social relationships and in associating with groups and communities. It is a catalyst to developing a sense of social responsibility, and helps to resolve conflicts with family members and friends. Sweet pea is good for those with several planets in Libra, especially Saturn, and for hard aspects between Jupiter and Saturn.

Quaking grass has a certain bending flexibility in its form and also is part of a group, rather than separate, as other grasses. It thus brings out group harmony and cooperation through the blending of individual egos. It is a helpful essence for those with Saturn in Libra, several planets in Libra or Aries, and hard aspects between Venus and Saturn.

Penstemon is found growing under the shady sides of rocks in harsh alpine terrains; it suggests a quality of strength in a difficult environment. It is helpful for those who tend to withdraw from relationships when they encounter obstacles and need the openness and confidence to work through their problems. This remedy may be called for by those with Venus-Saturn hard aspects and combinations of Moon/Saturn/Venus, Moon/Saturn/Pluto, or Moon/Saturn/Mars.

Goldenrod blooms at the time the Sun is in Libra. It is used for those who create interpersonal barriers or take on a false persona, who need to learn to be true to their deeper selves in social relationships. Goldenrod is useful for those with hard aspects between Venus and Saturn or Neptune, as well as for those with Saturn in Libra.

Red clover essence deals with the group ego versus the individual ego, helping to clear the aura of fear, hysteria, and panic absorbed from others. The fear and panic may also be from the collective unconscious or associated with Earth changes and not personal matters. Red clover brings an inner calm and peace with the ability to see the issues clearly. It may be called for by those with strong Libra planets or with Neptune transits.

SCORPIO

Scorpios need to transform their desire nature into a higher vibration, find their own spiritual center, release old emotional patterns, and understand their deep fears. When they are working on a positive vibration, Scorpios are constantly transforming emotions and catalyzing others to let go of their old habits.

Bach Remedies

Willow works with releasing resentment and bitterness, learning not to blame others and adverse circumstances for one's own misfortunes. It enables one to find optimism and faith while recognizing true responsibility in life's game. Willow may be useful for those with hard aspects between Pluto and the Moon or Mars as well as for transits of Pluto.

Holly helps to transform hatred, envy, and jealousy; it works with feelings of misunderstanding, insecurity, and suspicion. It can alleviate hostility between individuals and make them loving, tolerant of others, and inwardly happy and secure. It may be called for under certain Pluto transits, especially those of Venus, the Moon, and Mars.

Rock rose is an essence that works with states of terror and extreme fright as one may experience after an accident or violence. It enables one to have a deep sense of courage and to be willing to help others in danger. It is an excellent remedy to have on hand during Pluto and Uranus transits.

FES Remedies

Sagebrush (from the *Artemisia* genus, not garden sage of the *Salvia* mint genus) is used physically to "smoke" or purify environments. The *Artemisia* family, including mugwort and wormwood, is known for its magical dreamlike qualities. The essence is used to purify ourselves or rid ourselves of old patterns that we carry with us, letting go of some of the layers of the onion. It is a particularly good remedy to use under Pluto transits when we are undergoing major transformations in our personality. It is also effective on a short-term basis for clearing the energy of another person or environment.

Sticky monkeyflower (also known as Orange Bush Mimulus) helps to balance out sexual energy. For some, it is breaking free of repressions and emotional fears of intimacy; for others, it helps balance an obsession with sex. For many, it loosens blockages of the creative force or life energy. This remedy is helpful for those who have hard aspects from Pluto or Saturn to Venus, Mars, or the Moon.

Fuchsia works on releasing tensions from emotional blockages. Many emotional patterns are repressed in childhood and stay buried until such a time when the individual is ready to work with the events that triggered these reactions and repressions. This often happens during a Pluto transit or a transit to natal Pluto or Scorpio planets. Fuchsia then can be extremely helpful as a catalyst in releasing these old emotional barriers.

Basil has had a history of being associated with misfortune, curses, and poison. Nicholas Culpeper assigned it to Mars and Scorpio and commented that it draws out poisons from stings of wasps or hornets. It also has positive associations with the spiritual world in the East as a protective herb. Thus, basil seems to balance life's extremes and is associated with the transformation of death and birth, being both a painful poison and a healing herb. The essence of basil works with spirituality and sexuality in relationships. Basil is useful to those with hard aspects between Venus-Mars and Venus-Pluto and to those having transits of Pluto over their Moon, Venus, or Mars.

Garlic essence aids fear and insecurity, which paralyzes the individual will and drains the life force. It helps to release impurities and cleanse the being of these emotions. In similar fashion, garlic physically works to remove toxins and purify the blood. It is helpful for those with hard aspects between Pluto and Mars, Neptune, or the Moon.

Black-Eyed Susan is comprised of two basic parts—the elongated orange-yellow ray flowers and the black disk flowers in the center, likened to the inner darkness within the soul. The essence helps to penetrate inner darkness with conscious insight and begins to transform these emotions. It provides spiritual courage for those who fear looking within and uncovering buried emotions like anger and sadness. It is a remedy that is extremely useful under transits of Pluto to the Moon, Ascendant, Venus, Mars, and Saturn.

Trillium works to overcome greed and lust for power. The red bud of trillium reaches skyward in a prayerful gesture. This shows the ability to lift itself up from the darkness of the woods where it grows toward the light. Thus, the flower essence helps to transform baser instinct into selflessness, and enables one to let go of personal desires. It is helpful for those with strong Pluto or Scorpio planets and those undergoing transits of Pluto.

SAGITTARIUS

Sagittarians tend to be overexpansive, reaching out in too many directions at once, overindulging in food and drink, and are often dogmatic in terms of their ideas and philosophy. When balanced, a Sagittarian is optimistic and fun to be with, has a strong sense of justice, and is a wise and compassionate teacher.

Bach Remedies

Vervain is a good remedy for extremes of mental energy that often manifest in stress, tension, and overenthusiasm. It helps those who force themselves to do things beyond their physical strength. It also helps Sagittarians who possess strong opinions and ideas, which they often try to impose on others. Vervain brings a calmness and wisdom to those who are sure of their own ideas and open-minded to the ideas of others. It is especially good for those with hard aspects between Jupiter and Mercury, Uranus, or Mars.

Wild oat helps those who are ambitious but uncertain of which avenues they should pursue. They often feel dissatisfied and despondent. This remedy catalyzes them to focus on their ambitions and makes them feel useful and fulfilled. Wild oat may be used by those who have many planets in Gemini or

Sagittarius or have hard aspects between Mercury and Jupiter, Uranus and Jupiter, and Mercury and Uranus.

FES Remedies

Mountain pride is related to penstemon (see Libra). It grows in harsh conditions out of the mountain rocks, but its red color conveys its warriorlike strength and assertiveness in the face of obstacles. Its pride is like the Archer with his bow and arrow. It may be helpful for those with Saturn or Neptune in hard aspect to Jupiter or Mars.

Larkspur has a light and subtle quality with its blue-violet flowers. The botanical name for larkspur is *Delphinium depauperatum*. *Delphinium* comes from the Greek word for larkspur, which means "little dolphin" due to the shape of its nectary. The dolphins were considered teachers and leaders of the sea, helping to guide distressed ships back to safety. In like manner, the larkspur suggests high spiritual ideals of altruism and generosity with true qualities of leadership. It is a helpful essence for those with several planets in Sagittarius or with a strong Jupiter.

Hound's tongue (see Taurus) is a good remedy for overindulgence, which is a Jupiterian quality. It also brings out attributes of idealism and uplifts the mind. Hound's Tongue may be helpful for hard aspects from Venus or Neptune to Jupiter or for those with several planets in Sagittarius.

CAPRICORN

Capricorns tend to be too hard on themselves, overly disciplined, and unable to express the joy of life. They can become rigid in their patterns and fearful of letting go of old structures and ideas. They need to learn to be more flexible and play at living. They can also become severely depressed at times and despair of their plight. On a positive note, a Capricorn is practical and well organized. They constantly persevere to climb up the mountain of life and offer a helping hand to fellow travelers. They are good teachers, complete projects, and have a deep sense of humor.

Bach Remedies

Rock water is the only remedy of Dr. Bach's not made from a plant or tree. It reflects a state of mind that is hard and inflexible, requiring the soothing gentle drops of water to relax and release old patterns. High ideals and perfectionism need to be tempered and softened. With a flexible mind, high ideals will seek a greater truth and find inner peace. Rock water is helpful for those with a strong Capricorn or Virgo emphasis in their horoscope.

Elm balances out feelings of inadequacy and a striving for perfection. It gives self-assurance and confidence with an inner conviction of one's abilities. Elm may be helpful to those who have the Sun, Moon, or Ascendant in Capricorn, several planets in Capricorn, or a strongly placed Saturn.

Mustard aids those who feel deeply depressed and melancholic. It helps build an inner stability and joyfulness that can withstand attacks of despair or depression. This is often called for by those who have a Capricorn Sun or Moon with hard aspects to Saturn, or with hard aspects from Saturn to Venus. It is a useful remedy for transits of Saturn as well.

Oak is helpful for those who continue to persevere in the face of difficulties. They tend to overwork and to shoulder the responsibility of others, often hiding their own despondency. When they are in balance, they are courageous and strong as the tree itself with stability and hope. This is an excellent remedy for those who have a Capricorn emphasis in their horoscope or an angular Saturn; it is also helpful under Saturn transits.

Gentian works with those who have a negative outlook and suffer from depression. They lack the faith that would enable them to overcome certain difficulties, and thus they become despondent at setbacks. Their depression is different from that of those who need mustard in that it is from a known cause. When balanced, they can overcome any obstacle or take on any new tasks without feeling discouraged. This remedy may be called for with combinations of Saturn/Mars/Neptune, Saturn/Venus/Neptune, or Saturn/Mars/Pluto.

Gorse is for those who are utterly hopeless and in despair. They may have been suffering for a long time or have an illness that has given them little hope of recovery. It is also useful for those who have been told that they have some inherited condition that cannot be cured. In time, they can obtain a positive faith and understanding to surmount any difficulties. This is an important remedy under certain transits of Saturn and Pluto.

Sweet chestnut aids those who are going through the extremes of mental anguish and despair. Their despair is even more intense than that of those for whom gorse is recommended; they tend to keep it to themselves and often break under it. Using this remedy helps transform them to where they can ask for help and put their faith in a higher power. This is another important remedy for Saturn and Pluto transits and strong Saturnian individuals.

FES Remedies

Scotch broom is another remedy that works to alleviate despair and hope-lessness. Its bright yellow flower is uplifting, and its manner of taking over and spreading itself shows its strong purpose and tenacity in overcoming any obstacles in Nature. Likewise, on an emotional level, it holds its ground and awakens the strength in individuals to deal with difficulties and crises as challenges for growth. Scotch broom is a good remedy for those with a Capricorn Sun or Moon square Saturn and for those experiencing transits of Saturn or Pluto.

Saguaro flowers come from the giant saguaro cactus. The flowers bloom during the night but stay open the following day. Thus, the relationship between the power of the Moon, which works on them by night, and the power of the Sun is made manifest. The essence can help balance male/female energy within one and deal with authority or power. It puts one in touch with ancient and eternal truths and with underlying spiritual guidance. Saguaro is helpful for those with Sun-Saturn, Sun-Pluto, Sun-Moon, or Moon-Saturn hard aspects.

AQUARIUS

Aquarians can be detached, aloof, overly mental, and preoccupied with their ideas. The positive vibration of Aquarius is the innovative thinker and inventor, working to serve humanity through universal love. Aquarius can also be erratic and rebellious, breaking through structures and dogmas.

Bach Remedies

Walnut is helpful in breaking links with the past, leaving behind old patterns and friends while starting anew. In doing this, it is important to have a strong determination and to be unaffected by the opinions and beliefs of others. This is a very important remedy to use during the transits of Uranus and also during certain Pluto transits where old patterns are left behind and new paths begun.

Star of Bethlehem is used for the effects of shock (sudden bad news, accidents, deaths, etc.). It is one of the five remedies used in Dr. Bach's rescue remedy. It is most important to have this remedy on hand for all Uranus transits!

Vervain is an aid to the extremes of mental energy that often manifest as stress, tension, and overwork. Affected individuals tend to be high-strung and anxious. Vervain may bring about the calmness and wisdom of one who is willing to listen to the ideas of others. This is a good remedy for hard aspects of Uranus-Mercury and Uranus-Mars; it is also helpful during Uranus transits.

Water violet helps those who are proud and often feel superior to their peers. They are self-reliant and don't interfere in the affairs of others. When balanced, they are of great service to others and sympathetic wise counselors. This remedy is often called for by those who have strong Leo-Aquarius in their horoscopes or those who have hard aspects between the Sun and Uranus.

FES Remedies

Chamomile helps the nervous system and the "wired" feeling one often experiences when involved in a project, putting in many hours of work. It is a good remedy for a strongly placed Uranus and Mercury, for several planets in Aquarius, and for hard aspects of Uranus and Mercury. It is also helpful during Uranus transits.

Dill essence is useful in states of being overwhelmed by too much stimuli. It helps to create a calmer, more centered state of being and an ability to flow with life's changes. Dill is often called for by those with a strong Mercury or Uranus or several planets in Virgo, Gemini, and Aquarius. It's also beneficial during Uranus transits.

Self-heal essence enhances the awareness of one's own healing power. It is a catalyst to the process of physical healing, enabling individuals to accept all aspects of themselves and let go of suffering. It is often used in combination with other essences for centering and is added to oils and salves. Self-heal may be recommended for those under Uranus transits who are beginning to come into contact with their own abilities.

PISCES

Pisceans can be "wishy-washy" and indecisive, play the martyr role, and be oversensitive to their environment and to others. On a positive vibration, Pisces energy manifests as compassionate and loving, artistic and inspired, and full of selfless, healing energy.

Bach Remedies

Aspen aids in dispelling fears of unknown origin—terror that comes as a result of bad dreams, or anxieties that crop up inexplicably from time to time. It brings about a fearlessness and simple trust. Aspen is often needed by those with several planets in Pisces, the Moon in hard aspect to Neptune, or the Ascendant in hard aspect to Neptune. It's also beneficial during Neptune transits.

Clematis aids those who appear to be indifferent, dreamy, inattentive, and lacking in concentration. They have poor memories, are impractical, and are sensitive to all kinds of outside influences. The positive aspect of clematis is seen in those who have a lively interest in things and are sensitive without being "spaced out," such as writers, artists, and healers. Clematis is an important remedy for those having a strong Neptune influence or several planets in Pisces.

FES Remedies

Yarrow's botanical name, *Achillea millefolium,* comes from the Greek warrior Achilles, who used the herb to staunch the bleeding wounds of his soldiers. The Chinese use yarrow stalks in I Ching divination, and the Native Americans use it for purification in sweat lodge ceremonies. Yarrow essence protects against psychic harm from individuals or from environmental influences. Pink yarrow has a similar protective quality but a more emotional hue. Yarrow is helpful for those with hard aspects between Neptune and the Moon, Mars, the Ascendant, or the Midheaven, or with several planets in Pisces.

Star tulip is a type of mariposa lily that bears resemblance to a cat's ears. This suggests sensitivity and receptivity and thus the essence works to open to expanded consciousness. It is helpful for those ready to receive guidance from their higher selves to release any blockages and fears. Star tulip is a remedy that may be used by many during the transits of Neptune.

Manzanita essence works with grounding and balancing for those opening up to greater spiritual awareness. Manzanita flourishes in areas where other plants have a difficult time growing; therefore, it shows us how to handle the denser physical forms. Those needing manzanita often have difficulty accepting the physical body and the earth plane. For those with several planets in Pisces, an elevated Neptune, or hard aspects between Neptune and the Moon, Mars, or the Ascendant, this essence is often recommended.

Lotus has been used in Oriental spiritual tradition for thousands of years and is associated with spiritual unfoldment and the opening of the chakras. Lotus is used in combination with other essences to enhance the process of spiritual enlightenment. It is an excellent essence to use under Neptune and Pluto transits.

Aromatherapy and Planetary Correspondences

Aromatherapy, the use of aromas or essential oils, is an ancient form of alchemy that was correlated with astrology in the Middle Ages.

Aromas are subtle and may not have as strong an effect as herbs on the physical body; they do, however, affect the subtle bodies, which in turn affect the physical body.

Essential oils were used by the Egyptians who put them in cosmetics, massage oils, and medicines. The priests, and later the physicians, were the first to use the aromatics. The aromatics used in Egypt include myrrh, frankincense, cedarwood, origanum, bitter almond, spikenard, henna, juniper, coriander, calamus, and other indigenous plants. The Egyptians also used cedarwood oil in the process of mummification.

The ancient Hebrews used essential oils. Many of their religious rituals employed various oils, and women were given a twelve-month purification with myrrh oil.

Learning from the Egyptians, the Greeks attributed the origin of aromatics to the goddesses and gods; they used various oils to make perfumes and to anoint specific parts of the body. The Greek physicians recognized the difference between stimulating and sedative properties in the essences. The Romans were even more lavish in their use of perfumes than the Greeks.

The knowledge of distillation, however, had remained forgotten since Egyptian times. An Arabian physician known as Avicenna is credited with this invention in the tenth century. Avicenna first used the rose and later distilled other essences.

The Chinese used aromatics during acupuncture, and many essences are written about in the Hindu Ayurvedas. Sandalwood was used as an incense and an unguent.

In the Middle Ages, the herbalists and alchemists worked with essential oils and were familiar with the process of distillation. Perfumers who worked with these essences rarely succumbed to illness when cholera and other diseases were prevalent. This was because nearly all essential oils are good antiseptics.

In modern times, research has been carried out in regard to the antiseptic properties of essences. This research has been conducted primarily by chemists and pharmacists. René Maurice Gattefosse was a chemist interested in the cosmetic use of essences. He soon gathered enough information to convince him that many essential oils had even greater antiseptic properties than some of the antiseptic chemicals in use. One of Gattefosse's hands was badly burned as a result of a small explosion in his laboratory. He immersed it in lavender oil and found that the burn healed at a phenomenal rate with no infection or scarring. Gattefosse published his first book, *Aromatherapie*, in 1928.

A colleague of Gattefosse named Godissart set up an aromatherapy clinic in Los Angeles. He was successful in achieving cures for skin cancer, gangrene, osteomalacia (softening of the bones as a result of imbalance in calcium and phosphorus metabolism), facial ulcers, and bites from black widow spiders using lavender oil.

Meanwhile, another Frenchman, a medical doctor named Jean Valnet, began to use essences in his treatments. He used them during the war in treating battle wounds and in many pathological conditions. Dr. Valnet administered the oils orally—a few drops in a little sugar.

Marguerite Maury, a French biochemist and author of *The Secret of Life and Youth* (C.W. Daniel, 1989), used the oils in massage work so that they absorbed through the tissues of the body; in this way, they worked on internal organs as well. She found that bergamot, chamomile, and lavender stimulated the production of white blood cells when rubbed on the skin or inhaled.

Italy has also produced some researchers in this field. Doctors Gatti and Cajola, working in the 1920s and 1930s, realized the scope of therapy with essential oils. Paolo Roveti of Milan worked with citrus oils indigenous to Italy—bergamot, lemon, and orange—and also demonstrated clinically the benefit of certain essences in states of anxiety and depression.

Good methods of getting essential oils into the bloodstream, other than by taking them internally, are baths, inhalations, compresses, and massage.

Using Aromas with the Horoscope

Aromas may be used to strengthen a planetary energy where it is weak, meaning unaspected planets, planets receiving few aspects (unless they are angular), and sometimes planets that may be in the sign of their detriment or fall.

A planet that rules a sign is said to be **dignified** in that sign. For example, Mars is dignified in Aries. A planet is said to be in **detriment** in the sign opposite the one it rules; Venus would be in its detriment in Scorpio. In addition, there is one other sign where a planet is said to be **exalted** (where it also works well), and when the planet is in the sign opposite to this one it is said to be in its **fall** (where it does not work so well).

PLANETARY DIGNITIES				
Planet	Sign Ruled	Detriment	Exaltation	Fall
Sun	Leo	Aquarius	Aries	Libra
Moon	Cancer	Capricorn	Taurus	Scorpio
Mercury	Gemini	Sagittarius	Virgo	Pisces
	Virgo	Pisces		
Venus	Taurus	Scorpio	Pisces	Virgo
	Libra	Aries		
Mars	Aries	Libra	Capricorn	Cancer
	Scorpio	Taurus		
Jupiter	Sagittarius	Gemini	Cancer	Capricorn
	Pisces	Virgo		
Saturn	Capricorn	Cancer	Libra	Aries
	Aquarius	Leo		
Uranus	Aquarius	Leo	Scorpio	Taurus
Neptune	Pisces	Virgo	Cancer	Capricorn
Pluto	Scorpio	Taurus	—	—

This system of detriments, exaltations, and falls was used by the ancients. Today it seems more appropriate to speak of the positive or negative manifestations of a planet rather than simply its strength or weakness. The negative manifestations would include both a lack of that planet's energy and an excess of its energy. Generally, the aromas connected with the planet would be used when it is lacking in energy. The aromas connected with an opposite planetary energy are used to balance excess energy.

The negative use of **solar energy** might manifest as lowered vitality and an indefinite sense of one's individual worth. This could occur if the Sun is unaspected, in the twelfth house, or receiving a hard aspect from its ruler, as a Pisces Sun square Neptune. For enhancing the vital essence, one might use aromas such as melissa, benzoin, and patchouli.

Negative **Moon** energy might indicate an overly emotional person or one with a weak Moon who needs to stimulate the intuitive nature. The first condition might include a Moon with hard aspects from Mars or Jupiter; the second, an unaspected Moon or Moon with hard aspects from the Sun or Saturn. One could balance overly emotional qualities with the solar aromas and stimulate the emotional, intuitive nature or imagination through the use of the lunar aromas cypress or juniper.

Negative **Mercury** manifestations include an inability to communicate (Mercury-Saturn hard aspects) as well as an overly sensitive nervous system with respiratory problems (Mercury-Mars and Mercury-Uranus hard aspects). To help communication and retention of memory, rosemary and lavender are good essences. For nervousness or anxiety, Jupiterian aromas such as cedarwood and sandalwood might prove helpful.

Venus in its negative mode refers to blocked emotional energies—difficulty in expressing love and affection. This is often seen when Venus receives hard aspects from Saturn and sometimes from Mars or Pluto. One might also want to increase a sense of beauty or aesthetics. Aromas such as rose, bergamot, jasmine, and ylang-ylang might be appropriate. When there is too much Venusian softness, Martian aromas are helpful.

Negative **Mars** energy manifests either as extreme aggression with warlike traits or a lack of vitality, courage, and will. The first condition may occur with Mars in hard aspect to Pluto, the Sun, or Jupiter, or when Mars is angular. The second condition may occur with hard aspects from Saturn. In the first case, aromas associated with Venus are helpful as a balance in addition to those associated with Neptune (the higher vibration of Venus). For those who lack Mars energy, the essential oils basil, cinnamon, black pepper, and ginger would be helpful. (Ginger may also be drunk as a tea and cinnamon used as a culinary spice.)

The dark side of **Jupiter** is often viewed as restrictions in the ability for growth, expansion, and optimism. This can occur with hard aspects from Saturn in the horoscope. Jupiter can also be overexpansive, excessive, and indulgent, which may be a result of hard aspects from Neptune, Venus, or the Moon. Utilizing cedarwood or sandalwood essences might be beneficial for increasing Jupiterian qualities; working with the essences of Saturn would be helpful in limiting Jupiter's inflationary tendencies.

Saturnian energies in excess make individuals very crystallized and set in their ways. This may be a result of several planets in Capricorn, an angular Saturn or a strongly aspected Saturn. A lack of Saturn energy causes difficulty in assuming responsibility and discipline. This may be true of Saturn when it receives hard aspects from Neptune. The lunar essences cypress and juniper help to balance excess Saturnian qualities. The Saturnine essences pine and eucalyptus have the strength of the trees from which they derive and would impart the qualities of responsibility and discipline.

Uranus can bombard the nervous system with too much energy. This can occur with strong Uranus-Mercury or Uranus-Mars hard aspects. Solar aromas such as melissa and patchouli can help to ground this vigor. When the Uranian force is weak, as in an unaspected Uranus, or Uranus is in hard aspect to Saturn, more inspiration and excitement is needed. In these cases, Uranian/Mercurial essences like peppermint can be helpful.

Neptune manifests negatively in one being "spaced out" or ungrounded. This occurs when it makes hard aspects to the Moon, the Ascendant, or the Midheaven. In these cases, aromas ruled by Mercury (Mercury rules Virgo, the sign opposite to Pisces) would tend to accentuate the clear-thinking, analytical capacity and counterbalance mental vagueness. To increase higher Neptunian energy, inspiration, and intuition, aromas such as clary sage and myrrh would be helpful. Essences like these are often needed where the emphasis in the horoscope is overly analytical or mental, as with several planets in Gemini or Virgo or a strong Mercury.

Plutonian energy can be heavy, dark, and depressing with many planets in Scorpio or strong Pluto-Saturn hard aspects. One often turns to the aromas of

Venus (Venus rules Taurus, the opposite sign from Scorpio) for balance. However, when one needs to enhance the transformative catalytic qualities of Pluto, aromas such as sage, cedarwood, and sandalwood are helpful.

Planetary Rulership of Essential Oils

SUN

Essences ruled by the Sun have a stimulating, warming effect and are helpful to the circulatory system.

Melissa derives from the Greek word for "bee," an insect that is attracted by the scent of the leaves, which smell like lemons. In Southern Europe it is known as "heart's delight." It is one of the earliest medicinal herbs and was used by Paracelsus, who called it the "elixir of life." All the old herbalists spoke of melissa as a remedy for melancholy and strengthener of the nerves and brain. Melissa is a tonic rather than a stimulant; it strengthens the heart, nervous and digestive systems, and the uterus. For heart conditions, it is helpful for palpitations and when there is overstimulation or heat. On the nervous system it has an antispasmodic action and an uplifting, joyful effect. It is sedative and calming, slowing the respiration and lowering the pulse and blood pressure. Melissa oil resembles fennel and peppermint in its digestive carminative action. It is good for nausea, vomiting, and flatulence. Melissa has an affinity for the female reproductive system; it has a relaxing effect and therefore works well for cramps. It is also a mild emmenagogue and is used for menstrual irregularity and infertility.

Benzoin comes from a tree cultivated in Java, Sumatra, and Thailand. The gum is not naturally produced but forms when a deep incision is made in the trunk. A beautiful reddish brown resinoid is made from the gum. Benzoin was burned as an incense and used to drive away evil spirits in ancient times. It is best known in the form of tincture of benzoin, which is a strong inhalant for respiratory problems. Benzoin has a very stimulating, energizing action. It expectorates mucus, stimulates the urine flow, warms and tones the heart, and expels flatulence. When it is used with conditions as colds, coughs, asthma, or bronchitis, it may be taken internally or by inhalations. Externally, benzoin is of value in skin conditions where there is redness, irritation, or itching.

Neroli (Orange Blossom) is the oil distilled from the blossoms of bitter orange. Called oil of Neroli Bigarade, its name stems from the wife of a famous

Italian prince of Nerola who used it to perfume her gloves and her bath water in the sixteenth century. The orange tree comes from China, where the flowers have been used for centuries in cosmetic preparations. It is cultivated now in France, Tunisia, Italy, and the United States. Neroli oil is one of the finest oils; it has a pale yellow color and is blended with other fine oils to make an expensive Eau de Cologne. Neroli is one of the most effective antidepressant oils, being used for insomnia, hysteria, anxiety, and depression. It is calming to the mind and heart and is used for palpitations and cardiac spasm. Neroli is very beneficial for the skin; it acts on a cellular level, stimulating the elimination of old cells and the growth of new ones. It may be used where there is irritation or redness.

Patchouli comes from India and Indonesia and is a deep reddish brown color like myrrh. It became known in Great Britain in the 1820s when it was used to impregnate Indian shawls. It is used in small quantities in perfume and, along with camphor, in India ink. Like the Sun, patchouli is stimulating in small doses and sedative in large amounts. It is a very strong nerve stimulant and an excess of this aroma may keep one awake at night. Patchouli is also known as an aphrodisiac. It has the astringent properties of myrrh and is used for redness and dry skin. Also like myrrh, its odor is musty and sweet.

MOON

Lunar essences work with the female organs, are relaxing and calming, and increase the intuitive function.

Chamomile is one of the oldest known medicinal herbs. It has been regarded as the plant's physician because it was thought to keep other plants in good health. The fragrance of chamomile flowers is like apples, and thus it was called *kamai melon* (ground apple) by the Greeks. Of the number of species of chamomile, only one is commonly used in medicine. This is *anthemis novilis*, Roman chamomile. Another of the species, which has a smaller flower head and fewer petals, is known as German chamomile and is most commonly used as tea. Interest in chamomile has intensified recently because of the discovery that it contains azulene. Azulene, when isolated, is comprised of intense blue crystals and is an excellent anti-inflammatory agent. It is formed when the essential oil is distilled and is being used in a number of pharmaceutical preparations and toiletries. Azulene is more predominant in the German chamomile oil. Chamomile is strongly indicated for any internal or external inflammatory conditions; it is used for burns, conjunctivitis, dermatitis, gastritis, colitis, and nephritis. It has a mild antispasmodic action and is helpful in asthma and bronchitis. For digestive disorders, especially peptic ulcers, chamomile is excellent. It alleviates many female disorders, including painful menstruation, excessive loss of blood, vaginitis, and menopausal problems. It has a strong effect on the mind and the nervous system and is used for hysteria and nervous problems. Oil of chamomile is excellent for children's ailments due to its sedative action and low toxicity; it is used for oversensitivity, colic, diarrhea, spasms, teething, earaches, and other problems.

Cypress comes from a tall conical-shaped tree common to the Mediterranean region. It used to be worshipped on the island of its name. The oil has a woody quality with a bit of spice that resembles juniper and pine. Cypress oil is beneficial in conditions where there is excessive discharge of fluids; it is also good for hemorrhages, hemorrhoids, and varicose veins. It is useful for the female reproductive system, acting through the ovaries, and has been of value in menstrual disorders and during menopause.

Juniper is a small evergreen tree closely resembling cypress. It was used as an incense in early civilizations. In Tibet it was used for religious as well as medicinal purposes. As an aromatic shrub, it warded off evil spirits and served as a disinfectant in times of plague or other disease. The French burned a mixture of juniper twigs and rosemary leaves in hospital wards and sickrooms to purify the air. In Yugoslavia, juniper oil is used in traditional folk medicine. It makes a refreshing bath oil and is both stimulating and relaxing. Juniper oil has a slightly bitter taste and is one of the classic diuretics and remedies for urinary tract infections. It is also a good antiseptic for the respiratory and digestive tracts. It has a strengthening effect on the nerves and is a good treatment for nervous disorders and insomnia. Juniper is also useful externally for skin disorders as eczema and dermatitis.

MERCURY

Essences ruled by Mercury stimulate the respiratory and digestive systems. As Mercury rules two signs, Gemini and Virgo, many essences are included.

Cardamom comes from a plant that grows in India, Ceylon, and China. The oil has a sweet, spicy scent. It has a warming effect and principally affects the digestive system. It is often used in laxatives and as a treatment for colic. It helps to relieve nausea, as does peppermint, and is beneficial in relieving heartburn and intestinal gas. Psychologically, it is uplifting and is good for digestive problems of nervous origin. Externally, it makes an excellent, refreshing bath oil.

Fennel is related to aniseed and is thought to be indigenous to the shores of the Mediterranean. It was well known to the ancients and cultivated by the Romans. It has traditionally been used in cooking and was said to convey strength, courage, and longevity. Sweet fennel oil is one of the classic carminative remedies and is good for all digestive disorders. It is also an antispasmodic and may be useful for bronchitis and colic. Fennel is a good diuretic and should be given when there is insufficient excretion of urine. Fennel has always been used for obesity because of its hormonal action, and it is also utilized for menopausal problems and increasing mother's milk.

Lavender comes from the Latin word *lavare*, which means "to wash." It was used by the Romans in connection with their bathing activities. It is a principal ingredient in toilet water and in many sachets. Obtained from wild plants in France and cultivated plants in England and Tasmania, lavender is the most useful and most versatile oil. It is known for its nervine sedative properties and has proved valuable for depression, insomnia, migraines, hysteria, nervous tension, and paralysis. It is a heart tonic and calms the nerves of the heart; thus, it is recommended for palpitations and tremblings. A powerful skin rejuvenating agent, it is effective for eczema, dermatitis, acne, psoriasis, and burns. Lavender is soothing for inflammations and is one of the most effective oils for stimulating circulation.

Rosemary is one of the most renowned herbs throughout history. Sprigs of rosemary were used to drive away evil spirits; it was burned as an incense and fumigant in sickrooms. Rosemary water is one of the main ingredients of Hungary water (named after Queen Elizabeth of Hungary), a rejuvenating lotion. Rosemary oil will relieve a headache when applied to the temples. The oil has a warm, sharp taste similar to camphor. It is a good nerve stimulant and is used in disorders where there is a reduction or loss of nerve function, as in paralysis or loss of speech. It is also an excellent heart tonic, good for cardiac disorders such as palpitations.

Thyme is used in cooking and as a medicine. It contains thymol, which is a strong antiseptic. Thyme stimulates the production of white corpuscles in the blood during infectious diseases. It is also an excellent nerve tonic for headaches, anxiety, depression, and insomnia.

Peppermint is one of the most widely used oils as a flavoring in commercial sweets and toothpastes. The Greeks and Romans crowned themselves with peppermint besides using it to flavor sauces and wines and adding it to their medicines. It is cultivated now in many parts of the world though native to the Mediterranean. Menthol, its principal constituent, has both sedative, cooling effects and warming effects. Its action on the digestive tract is the most pronounced; peppermint is a prime remedy for indigestion, flatulence, diarrhea, nausea, and vomiting. It is helpful for headaches and migraines related to digestion.

VENUS

Aromas under the rulership of Venus often come from flowers with very sweet smells. These oils are used to enhance one's aesthetic sense, and some of them are helpful for female problems and the skin, which is partly ruled by Venus.

Bergamot oil comes from the rind of a fruit that grows in Italy. Its scent is sweet and citrusy, and it has a strong floral quality. Along with neroli and lavender, it is one of the principal ingredients of the classic Eau de Cologne. Bergamot oil has been used in Italian folk medicine for fevers and worms. It is successfully used in douches and hip baths for gonococcal infections and vaginal discharges. Bergamot is useful for eczema, psoriasis, and other skin diseases. It is a nerve sedative, valuable in countering depression and anxiety.

Geranium oil comes from an aromatic plant and has a sweet scent. It is a mild analgesic and sedative; it is used for neuralgia and pain of nervous origin. As an antiseptic, it is good for burns, wounds, and ulcers and reduces inflammation. Like basil and rosemary, it stimulates the adrenal cortex and thus is used to balance hormones during conditions like menopause. The oil is of great value in skin care; it is astringent and may be used for inflamed skin as well as for congested, oily skin.

Jasmine oil has an exquisite scent; its use in many of the costliest perfumes make it one of the most expensive of the essences. In China, it is known as *moli* and used for scenting tea; the Hindus call it "moonlight of the grove." The oil is a deep reddish brown that blends well with rose and citrus oils. Jasmine oil works primarily on the emotional level and is of great value in psychological and psychosomatic problems, in that it is very uplifting and produces a feeling of optimism, confidence, and euphoria. It also has an effect on the female reproductive system. It relieves uterine spasms and menstrual pains.

It helps in relieving the pain of childbirth and in promoting the flow of breast milk. It is warming and relaxing to the body and is used in treating impotence and frigidity.

Rose is another of the most costly of the aromatics. The Greeks believe the rose to have sprung from the blood of Adonis. The Turks say it was the blood of Venus, and the Mohammedans claim it sprang from the sweat of Mohammed. Rose oil was accidentally discovered in Persia when a canal was filled with rose water at a wedding. The heat of the Sun caused the oil to separate and rise to the top. Persian rose oil is no longer commercially significant; the finest rose oil comes from Bulgaria, where it is extracted from the damask rose and known as Bulgarian rose otto.

Rose oil is used for disorders of the genito-urinary system—it regulates menstruation, is a gentle emmenagogue, and cleanses the womb of impurities. It is a known aphrodisiac and is said to increase semen. The cardiovascular system also benefits by the use of rose oil; it promotes circulation, cleanses the blood, and regulates the action of the spleen and heart. Rose oil acts strongly on the digestive system; it strengthens the stomach and promotes the flow of bile. A study in 1972 in Russia showed that rose oil may stimulate hepatic bile formation, especially the synthesis of bile acids and phospholipids. Rose oil is also one of the most antiseptic of the oils and is good for the skin, both for dryness as well as for redness and inflammation.

Ylang-ylang is obtained from the ylang-ylang tree, which has beautiful yellow flowers and is cultivated in Java, Sumatra, Réunion, Madagascar, and the Philippines. The finest oil comes from Manila in the Philippines. Its name means "flower of flowers," and it has an exotic scent similar to a mixture of jasmine and almond. Ylang-ylang affects the nervous system and is used as a sedative in states of anxiety, tension, and high blood pressure. It also has a euphoric effect. It relieves tachycardia and hyperpnea (abnormally fast breathing). Ylang-ylang is a good aphrodisiac and may be useful for impotence and frigidity. It has a soothing effect on the skin and is used in bath oils and facial massage oils.

MARS

Aromas ruled by Mars are stimulating and warming; they aid the circulatory and digestive systems.

Basil comes from the Greek *basilicon*, which means a "royal ointment or remedy." Basil is called *tulsi* in India and used extensively in Ayurvedic medicine. The essence has a light, refreshing odor and tastes sweet and slightly bitter. Basil resembles peppermint in many ways; it is good for indigestion and vomiting and is an antispasmodic useful for asthma, bronchitis, and sinus congestion. Oil of basil is the best nerve tonic; it gives the mind strength and clarity. It is used in such nerve disorders as hysteria, epilepsy, and paralysis. In Ayurvedic medicine, the juice of the leaves is given for colds and flus; it brings about perspiration, reduces fevers, and acts as an expectorant. The juice is also given to those who have been bitten by a snake. It acts as a rejuvenator and gives a glow to the complexion. In a bath, basil oil is refreshing, but it has both a hot and cold feeling and seems to sting the skin like a pinprick. (Culpeper gives it the rulership of Mars and says it comes under the sign of the Scorpion.)

Black Pepper, one of the oldest known spices, was used in India over 4,000 years ago. It was also used in ancient Greece and Rome. Black peppercorns are the sun-dried red berries that are picked from the plant before they are ripe. (White peppercorns are from the same plant, but the berries are not picked until they are fully ripe, and the outer layer is removed before drying.) Oil of black pepper is a light amber color and smells like clove oil. It has an energizing action on the digestive tract and is used in constipation, flatulence, and loss of appetite. It stimulates the respiratory system and urination. It restores tone to the musculature for a prolapsed colon or uterus. As a warming essence, black pepper is good for colds, flu, and fevers. It stimulates circulation, acts as a tonic to the spleen, and is an antitoxic agent in certain types of food poisoning. Externally, it is an analgesic, good for muscular aches and pains, toothache, or angina. As a stimulant, it is helpful for rheumatoid arthritis and paralysis.

Ginger has been known through the ages as a stimulant. It was used in ancient China and in India for its medicinal properties. Essence of ginger is good for digestive complaints as flatulence, dyspepsia, loss of appetite, and diarrhea. Ginger works well for nausea and is commonly taken on airplane flights to combat air sickness. It is used as a gargle for throat infections and tonsillitis and applied externally for rheumatoid arthritis.

JUPITER
Essences ruled by Jupiter are uplifting to the spirit and are often used in religious ceremonies.

Cedarwood oil comes from the Lebanon cedar; the wood was used in building temples and palaces in the Middle East and the Temple of Solomon in Jerusalem. Cedarwood oil was the first oil to be extracted from a plant for use by the Egyptians in the mummification process and in cosmetics. Cedarwood oil acts primarily on the skin and the respiratory and genito-urinary tracts. It is given when there is pain, burning, or difficulty in urinating, and it is a valuable remedy for cystitis. It affects the mucous membranes and is good in catarrhal conditions like coughs and bronchitis. It is also a sedative and is used for anxiety and nervous tension. Cedarwood oil has a strong effect on the skin; it is an astringent and an antiseptic and relieves itching. It is good for acne, oily skin, and dandruff, and may be valuable for eczema, dermatitis, and psoriasis, besides acting as an insect repellent.

Sandalwood oil comes from the sandalwood tree, which grows in East India and the Lingnan region of China. From earliest times, it has been in use as an incense and as an ingredient in embalming and cosmetics. In ancient India, it was employed in religious ceremonies and is mentioned in the "Nirukta," the oldest Vedic commentary known. In Egypt and China, it was also used as a perfume and an ingredient in cosmetics. The scent of sandalwood is sweet and spicy, akin to rose. Its taste is extremely bitter, which makes it a stimulus to digestion and to increasing the flow of bile. Because sandalwood has a strong action on the mucous membranes of the genito-urinary system and pulmonary tracts, it is used for chronic infections of these areas. In genito-urinary conditions where there is a mucous discharge (as in gonorrhea), sandalwood oil is appropriate. It is effective against streptococcus and staphylococcus, and with its antispasmodic property, it is also used for bronchitis and coughs. Externally, oil of sandalwood is one of the most useful for the skin. It aids dry skin and dehydrated skin as a warm compress; it also relieves itching and inflammation.

SATURN

Essences ruled by Saturn are basically yin and cooling though they also have the effect of being yang and warming when used in conditions such as rheumatism and arthritis.

Camphor is obtained from large hardy evergreen trees indigenous to China and Japan, but is also cultivated in India, Ceylon, and other subtropical countries. Camphor is present in every part of the tree but takes many years to form; it is drawn from the branches by chipping the wood and then boiling it in water. The camphor rises to the surface and becomes solid as the water cools. The oil is extracted by steam distillation and has a scent similar to that of eucalyptus. Camphor has its yin and yang qualities. Its action on the skin is cooling and anti-inflammatory. It is good for fevers, rheumatic inflammation, and burns. It also stimulates the heart and respiration and raises low blood pressure. Camphor useful as an inhalant for coughs, colds, bronchitis, and difficult breathing. It has a balancing effect on many yin and yang conditions: it stimulates depression and sedates hysteria; it activates digestive juices and is helpful in constipation, but it is also good for diarrhea, colic, and flatulence. Camphor is one of the more toxic essences and should be used with caution; in large doses it will cause convulsions.

Eucalyptus oil comes from the Eucalyptus tree, one of the tallest trees in the world. Indigenous to Australia, its name comes from the Greek *eucalypos*, meaning "well covered" because the flower buds are covered with a membrane that is thrown off as the flower expands. Eucalyptus oil is a good inhalant and chest rub; it has an odor like camphor and a bland bitter taste. It is excellent for all types of fever and conditions such as influenza, scarlet fever, and diphtheria since it has a strong cooling effect on the body; it is also one of the best antiseptic oils. Known for its action on the respiratory tract, eucalyptus is an expectorant and antispasmodic used for sinusitis, tuberculosis, and throat infections where there is a heavy mucus discharge. It is also a rubefacient and is applied externally for muscular and rheumatic pains while being a systemic remedy for rheumatoid arthritis because of its mild astringent effect.

Pine is found in the northern regions of Russia and Scandinavia; some of the best pine oil comes from northeast Russia and the Tyrol mountains of Austria. Pine is used in soaps and detergents because of its strong antiseptic properties. For all infections of the respiratory tract—bronchitis, asthma, and pneumonia—pine is excellent. It also works well for urinary infections, such as cystitis, and for inflammation of the gallbladder and gallstones. Externally, pine is used for rheumatic complaints and gout as well as for pulmonary diseases, sinusitis, and influenza.

URANUS

Aromas ruled by Uranus are sedative to the nervous system and antispasmodic.

Hyssop oil is golden yellow and fairly expensive; obtained from plants in Provence and Germany, it is used in perfumes and liqueurs. The Hebrews called this plant *Ezob*, and it is mentioned in the Bible. "Purge me with hyssop and I shall be clean." (Psalm 51:7) It has a hot bitter taste and clears the mind quickly, giving a feeling of alertness and clarity. One of the main uses for hyssop is for disorders of the respiratory tract; it promotes expectoration, relieves bronchial spasms, is an excellent cough remedy, and of great benefit for asthma and all catarrhal conditions. Hyssop acts as a mild sedative on the nervous system and as a nerve tonic, strengthening the nerves and bringing a feeling of relaxation. Hyssop also regulates blood pressure and is a general tonic for the cardiovascular system.

Marjoram oil is distilled from the flowering heads of sweet marjoram; the plant grows in Spain, southern France, and Tunisia. It was used in ancient times by the Egyptians; the Greeks used it in medicines, perfumes, and other toiletries. The name may possibly derive from the Greek *margaron*, which means "pearl." Marjoram, like basil, has a more refined scent than most of the essential oils; its taste is extremely bitter, warming the heart and stomach. Marjoram oil has a sedative effect. It relieves spasms, lowers high blood pressure, and stimulates the parasympathetic nervous system. The antispasmodic warming effect makes it a special ingredient in massage oils. It is very comforting for grief and emotional unrest. Marjoram acts as a laxative by stimulating intestinal peristalsis; it relieves intestinal spasms and is useful for colic and flatulence. Externally, marjoram is used for muscle spasms, rheumatic pains, sprains, and strains.

NEPTUNE

Essences ruled by Neptune have a euphoric and uplifting effect on one's being; they are also used in rituals and for spiritual enhancement. Essences listed under the Moon and Jupiter could also be included here.

Clary Sage is similar in appearance to common sage, but its blue flowers are slightly smaller. The name clary stems from the Latin *sclarea*, which derives from *clarus*, meaning "clear." This name originated from the fact that a mucilage is made from the seeds for clearing the eyes of foreign objects. Russia has the highest output of clary sage oil though small amounts are produced in southern France and Morocco. In Germany, clary is known as muscatel sage since it was used by German wine makers to simulate muscatel wine. Clary oil does slow one down and brings on a feeling of euphoria. The oil has a more pleasant floral quality than common sage; its taste is warm and bitter. Clary is a good nerve tonic for depression and is also beneficial for weak, fearful types of personalities. It produces a mild increase in blood pressure and is a good tonic for the female system. Clary sage is also known to strengthen the kidneys and stomach.

Frankincense was used in Egypt thousands of years ago in making rejuvenating face masks, cosmetics, and toiletries. In the form of incense, it was used to fumigate the ill in order to drive out the evil spirits. Frankincense derives its name from the French *francensens*, which means "luxuriant incense." It was considered one of the most prized substances of the ancient world, and according to the legend, was therefore offered to the Christ child, along with myrrh and gold. The gum comes from a small tree that grows in Arabia and Somaliland. Like many of the other gum essences, frankincense has a strong effect on the mucous membranes and is a good expectorant. As an inhalant or taken internally, it is used for catarrhal conditions of the head, lungs, stomach, or the intestines. Its astringent properties make it useful in hemorrhages, especially uterine or pulmonary. Externally, it is good for wounds, ulcers, and carbuncles in the same way as myrrh. Like benzoin, it has an elevating and soothing effect on the mind and emotions.

Myrrh is a gum resin that comes from the trunk of the myrrh bush, a small, hardy bush that is most commonly found in northeast Africa and southern Arabia. It was used in ancient times as an incense, perfume, and medicinal ingredient. The Egyptians burned it at noon as part of their Sun-worshipping ritual (its color is reddish brown); they also used it for embalming and in facial masks. Myrrh oil is helpful as a cosmetic ingredient because of its ability to preserve the flesh. It has a slightly cooling effect on the skin. The Book of Esther says that six of the twelve months devoted to the purification of women were accomplished with oil of myrrh. In ancient Greece, myrrh oil was used in one of the finest perfumes, known as *megaleion*. It was applied to battle wounds to promote healing and to reduce inflammation. According to Greek legend, myrrh was supposed to have originated from the tears of Myrrha, daughter of Cinyrus, King of Cyprus, who had been metamorphosed into a shrub. Myrrh oil is stimulating and strengthens the pulmonary system. It is a good expectorant for colds and coughs; it is also used for ulcers, gangrene, pyorrhea, and other conditions where there is wasting and degeneration.

PLUTO

Essences ruled by Pluto are cleansing and purifying; some of them are also beneficial for the female reproductive system.

Sage has many species, is found around the world, and is therefore one of the most common medicinal herbs. It has a restorative effect on the whole body, working with the digestive organs and the liver. It is also a stimulant to the nervous system and the adrenal cortex. Used as an emmenagogue for dysmenorrhea and menopausal difficulties, sage is also helpful for dyspepsia, loss of appetite, and nervous afflictions such as tremors, dizziness, and paralysis. Externally, it is used in vaginal douches, for insect bites, in gum care in cases of gingivitis, and for sore throats and laryngitis.

Cedarwood is used for cleansing and purifying the aura and environments. (See Jupiter.)

Sandalwood is used for embalming and as an incense for purification. (See Jupiter.)

Pennyroyal is a species of mint found in most parts of Europe. Its oil is similar to peppermint in taste and odor except that it is more bitter. It is basically warming and promotes perspiration. Pennyroyal is a good emmenagogue but should not be taken by pregnant women as it may cause abortion. A uterine tonic, pennyroyal is helpful for irregular menstruation, dysmenorrhea, and enhancing fertility. Pennyroyal also strengthens the nerves and has a slight analgesic effect; it is therefore valuable for nervous disorders and neuralgia. In fevers it promotes sweating and reduces one's temperature; in colds and coughs it expectorates mucus and relieves spasms. Externally, it has great value as an insect repellent, a topical for bites and stings of insects, and as a cleanser of blemishes because it promotes blood circulation.

Jasmine is used for the reproductive system in relieving menstrual cramps and the pains of childbirth. (See Venus.)

Ylang-ylang is useful for impotence and frigidity. (See Venus.)

Unification Rituals for Full Moons, Equinoxes and Solstices

To make Holistic Astrology more potent, we need to find practical ways to utilize cosmic cycles and to implement our own transformative energies to create healing on the personal, interpersonal, and planetary levels. Through ritual, we can connect with the subtle energies on the planet, our own universal selves, and the universal selves of all species. Ritual is communication with Earth Mother and Sky Father; it is the synthesis of natural cycles with our personal energy. Ritual opens us up to the subtler vibrations—the Great Mystery, the Goddess/God, the Divine in its many forms. Ritual helps to unite our rational, left-brain intelligence with our intuitive, right-brain creative intelligence.

Rituals can be done alone or in groups.

It is important in ritual work to choose a special harmonious place—outdoors where it is quiet, where natural forces contribute to the energy, and where a fire and circle may be made, or indoors where there is space to create a circle around a center of energy such as a hearth or altar. On this altar, indoors or out, it is vital to have some objects like candles or crystals that focus energy, as well as parts of birds or animals (feathers or bones) with whose spirits the person or group feels aligned. Some purifying herb as sage, cedar, sweetgrass, or incense to cleanse the space and clear each person's aura should be set out in addition to objects representing the four directions. It is good to have drums, rattles, and other musical instruments around to help bring in the energies; the drum represents the heartbeat of the Earth Mother.

If the ritual is being done in a group, the leader smudges everyone (burns sage, cedar, or sweetgrass and clears each person's aura) and calls in the four directions. In Native American rituals, a feather is used to symbolize the East (air), a candle or fire for the South (fire), water for the West (water), and pollen for the North (earth). In Wiccan ceremonies, the athame or sword represents the East; the wand (a branch of willow or oak), the South; the cup or chalice, the West; and the pentacle or five-pointed star, the North. Animals and birds representing the four directions are the eagle, East; the mouse, South; the black bear, West; and the buffalo, North.

Lunar Cycles and Full Moons

As we learn to balance our bodies through attuning to the larger planetary cycles, we become more sensitive to the monthly lunar cycles. Each month the Moon goes through various phases—New Moon, a seed time for new ideas and projects; First Quarter, a time to manifest new projects; Full Moon, a time of completion and fulfillment as well as sharing with others; Third Quarter, a time of understanding the meaning of the project and its contribution to one's growth and developing consciousness; and the dark of the Moon before New Moon, a time to let go of old ideas, transform energy, meditate, and bring in new awareness.

In all cultures, the Moon symbolizes the feminine force and is personified by the Goddess in her three aspects as Maiden, Mother, and Crone. The waxing Moon is the Maiden or daughter—Persephone, Diana, Venus, or Astarte; the Full Moon represents the Mother—Demeter, Ishtar, Yemaya; and the waning Moon, the Crone or Wisewoman—Hecate or Kali.

It is important to conduct rituals as close as possible to the time of the event—Full Moon, equinox, or solstice.

Full Moon in Aries (*Sun in Libra*)
Set up the altar or ceremonial place with red candles and stones such as carnelian, bloodstone, and garnet. Use these stones to get in touch with your inner strength. Ask yourself how you deal with anger. Do you hold back aggressive

tendencies or express them assertively? Aries/Libra is a time to balance the Martian/Venusian polarity.

Aries/Libra is also a time for balancing relationships. Are you too self-centered and too dominating in your relationships? You may need to temper these qualities. Flower remedies as heather and vine can be helpful for this.

If you are alone, climb a mountain or take a hike to see how your physical body reflects your inner strength and vitality. To bring out your Martian energy, the flower essences trumpet vine, cayenne, and Indian paintbrush are appropriate. Or try listening to music like Rossini's *William Tell Overture*, Sousa's Marches, or Kay Gardner's tape *A Rainbow Path*, which has music for each of the chakras.

Full Moon in Taurus *(Sun in Scorpio)*

This is close to All Hallows Eve, so costumes may be incorporated into the ritual. Sea-green or turquoise colors or candles may be used with stones such as malachite, emerald, chrysolite, and aventurine.

All can share which aspects of their personality they want to let go of (Scorpio) and which new aspects they want to manifest (Taurus). To break out of "stuck places," the flower remedies chestnut bud, chicory, and tansy may be helpful. For those wanting to express the higher aspects of the Venusian love vibration, essences of iris or California wild rose may be used.

If you are celebrating this lunation alone, make a list of old habits you want to shed and transformations you want to take place within your being. Enjoy the Venusian aspects of this lunation by listening to some music like Copland's *Fanfare for the Common Man* or the earthy songs of Buffy St. Marie or Odetta. A trip to an art museum may enhance the Taurean energies with paintings of Rubens, Renoir, or Gauguin.

Full Moon in Gemini *(Sun in Sagittarius)*

The Gemini Full Moon can be a time of scattered energies, so focusing on specific projects for the winter months is helpful. Setting up the ceremonial place with agate, cat's-eye, or tiger's-eye will help you attune to clear-sightedness. Flower remedies such as white chestnut, madia, or shasta daisy can aid your concentration.

Each person in the circle can share how to communicate with more people and spread the Sagittarian ideals and wisdom. Reading poems one has written and singing songs one has written are appropriate in celebrating this lunation.

If you are alone, write down ways in which you can focus your energy, including projects you might take on to share wisdom and knowledge. Read aloud some poetry and try expressing your own feelings in poetic form.

Full Moon in Cancer *(Sun in Capricorn)*
In your special ritual place use colors of silver and blue and stones like opal, moonstone, and pearl.

Do a Moon ceremony by invoking Grandmother Moon and the ancient Moon goddesses as Diana and Astarte to increase the creative feminine energies available on the planet at this time.

The Cancer Full Moon is a good time to let go of old emotional attachments and bring more balance and objectivity into one's life. The flower essences chicory and honeysuckle help to do this. It is also a time to bring out the Earth Mother nurturing qualities; pomegranate and mariposa lily can aid in grounding this vibration in the body.

If you are alone, go out and do a ceremony to the Moon; see where you need to increase your own creative and intuitive powers. Listen to some soothing and nurturing music, such as Handel's *Water Music*, Debussy's *Clair de Lune*, or the songs of Leonard Cohen.

Full Moon in Leo *(Sun in Aquarius)*
On the altar or fire circle, place some gold candles and a citrine crystal, topaz, or amber. Burn some myrrh or patchouli incense.

This lunation could be celebrated at sunrise with a morning Sun meditation, facing East and concentrating on the light and energy that the Sun brings. Face the East and feel the warmth of the Sun radiating in each of the chakric centers. Experience the centers where you need more light and warmth. (If there is no Sun out, you can do this indoors visualizing the Sun in your mind's eye.)

Next, look inside your heart (Leo rules the heart) to see if there are any people from whom you are withholding emotions. Send them healing and love and see the old restraining bonds dissolve. Hold hands and each of you share the inner feelings and emotions you are experiencing.

Utilize some chants and songs that bring out the Leo energy. *Let Me Be One with the Infinite Sun* is appropriate.

Let Me Be One with the Infinite Sun

Let me be one with the Infinite Sun
Forever and ever and ever
Let me be one with the Infinite Sun
Forever and ever and ever.
Hu a ke lano lano
Mau a te
Hi a nor Hi a nor Hi a nor
Hu a ke lano lano,
Mau a te
Hi a nor Hi a nor Hi a nor

For an individual celebrating this lunation alone, you might work with your own qualities of courage and strength and your use of power. Perhaps you need one of the flower remedies of Leo (sunflower, nasturtium, or dandelion) to aid you in manifesting your Leonian qualities. You might paint a picture reflecting the solar energy or listen to some music like Beethoven's *Fifth Symphony* that brings out the strength of Leo.

Full Moon in Virgo (*Sun in Pisces*)

Around the fire or altar place some brown candles and gems as tiger's-eye and earthy-colored agates. After calling in the four directions, call forth the spirit of the flowers and the plants that are preparing to burst forth from underneath the ground. Ask that they bring new energy and healing to the Earth Mother. Chants like "The Earth is Our Mother" might be sung. (See the section on Summer Solstice, page 169, for the words.)

Go around the circle, with all sharing how they can be more of service and less judgmental. Have everyone observe the ways in which they are overly critical of themselves. Experience the compassionate energy of the Pisces Sun and integrate it into your own life.

A good chant is the following:

I Will Be Gentle with Myself

I will be gentle with myself,
I will love myself,
I am a child of the Universe, We are one together.
(from the tape "The Giveaway" produced by the Ojai Foundation)

If you are celebrating this lunation alone, you can anoint yourself with some oil like rosemary or fennel. Think of the ways that you are too judgmental in your own life; you might make yourself a flower essence from beech, crab apple, corn, or dill. Play some songs to the Goddess or paint a picture of the Earth just before spring. Experience how the Earth feels, and try writing a poem or some prose.

Full Moon in Libra *(Sun in Aries)*

A few days before the Full Moon, do a spring cleansing and fast using some kidney herbs such as uva ursi, alfalfa, and nettles.

On the altar or around the fire put some spring herbs and any flowers that are in bloom. Add an aquamarine or green aventurine crystal, an emerald, or a malachite.

This is the time of Easter and the Jewish Passover celebration. Do a meditation on the symbolism of the resurrection of the Christ spirit and the Jews crossing the Red Sea in their deliverance from bondage. Think about that part of yourself that is still fettered. Share this with the others. Do some prayers for all those people on the planet who are still in some kind of bondage, physical or spiritual.

If you are celebrating this lunation alone, think of the relationships you are involved in and how you can bring them into balance. Should you give more or less to others in your relationships? What is it that needs to be changed in your relationship with others? You might want to make yourself one of the Libra flower remedies such as penstemon, sweet pea, or quaking grass to help bring relationships into balance.

Full Moon in Scorpio *(Sun in Taurus)*

This is an important Full Moon, known as the Wesak Full Moon in Buddhist cultures and is the time for celebration of Buddha's birthday.

The middle degree of each of the fixed signs (Taurus, Leo, Scorpio, Aquarius) is associated with one of the four portals or gates, each represented with an animal symbol (bull, lion, eagle, and man). These are mentioned in the Book of Revelation and other apocalyptic literature. Scorpio is the eagle, and the eagle soars above, overlooking his territory below. We have the opportunity at the Scorpio Full Moon to move to a transpersonal dimension, to begin anew. (The eagle represents the East or new beginnings in many Native American mythologies.)

You may use black candles and smoky quartz crystals, black obsidian, and jet to perform this ritual. It is important to place the smoky quartz so that the light shines through it. Since this is also the time near May Day, the celebration of fertility rituals and the richness of spring, lush spring wildflowers should be strewn around.

Burn some sage or cedar to purify everyone, and use oil of cedar for anointing. Scorpio Full Moon is a strong time to purify and release old patterns. Do a meditation on what it is that each person needs to let go of and transform. Have all share what this is and how they foresee converting the energy.

Share the richness of spring through chants to the Earth Mother, dance, and other joyous expressions. Prepare a salad of fresh spring herbs and other foods from plants that are in their spring abundance.

If you are alone, you might listen to some transformative music such as R. Strauss' *Death and Transfiguration*, Opus 24. Make a list or say aloud the things that you want to release. Examine areas in your life where you block your emotional or sexual energy. One of the Scorpio flower remedies as sticky monkeyflower, fuchsia, or Black-Eyed Susan may be helpful.

Full Moon in Sagittarius (*Sun in Gemini*)

For focusing the Sagittarian energy, give everyone a few drops of vervain or wild oat (flower remedies). Since Jupiter, ruler of Sagittarius, rules travel and foreign countries, people might dress in costumes from different countries for this ritual. They can share what is happening in that country and what it is that is important to be healed at this time. Songs from or about the country can also be sung.

Have all share how they can expand their inner knowledge and wisdom at this time. How can we contribute to planetary healing?

If you are alone, you might incorporate turquoise and chrysocolla and use them during the hour ruled by Jupiter. (See Jupiter stones in the chapter on crystals and gems.) You can burn incense such as melissa or sandalwood. Listen to uplifting music, perhaps Beethoven's *Ninth Symphony* or Sibelius' *Finlandia*, Opus 26. (This piece awakened the Finns to resist the Russian invasion.) The songs of John Denver or spirituals sung by Mahalia Jackson or Marian Anderson are other inspirational pieces.

Full Moon in Capricorn *(Sun in Cancer)*

At this time of the Summer Solstice and the beginning of summer, send healing to the Earth and pour water on her to help her through the dry season.

Brown and black stones like some agates, onyx, and jet may be placed around the ceremonial center. Candles of browns, oranges, and other Earth colors may be burned.

All present can share how they plan to manifest their energy in new projects through the summer months. Capricorn is a good time for setting the stage for new ideas and plans to organize them.

Examine any aspects of your being where you are stuck or crystallized. Share these with others and make a flower remedy of rock water, blackberry, or saguaro to help you flow with the energies as they are released.

If you are alone celebrating this lunation, make a list of your new ideas and projects. Listen to music by Haydn or Mozart or some of Schubert's symphonies to understand the organizational principles of Capricornian creativity.

Full Moon in Aquarius *(Sun in Leo)*

This is a time when the Sun is the hottest and Sun Dances are done by many Native American people. The blue crystals and gems aquamarine, azurite, lapis, and sapphire can be used to cool the heat of the Sun and to calm the Uranian vibrations.

All in the circle can share how they can bring in more light and love and what can personally be done in the way of humanitarian projects.

It might be helpful to use flower remedies such as chamomile, dill, and vervain to deal with the Uranian energy.

If you are alone during this lunation, write down your new ideas and endeavors. Think of ways you can inspire people to work for collective goals. For true Uranian inspiration, listen to the music of Stravinsky or Bartok, or play the songs of Bob Dylan, Joan Baez, or the New Troubadours.

Full Moon in Pisces *(Sun in Virgo)*

This is the beginning of the harvest season and a good time to do rituals for the gathering of Earth's bounty. Prayers and ceremonies to the Earth Mother are appropriate for honoring her and giving forth her abundance.

Purple candles can be set on your ceremonial place with amethyst and fluorite crystals to attune to the Piscean energy.

All present can share how they can increase personal inner awareness and manifest more compassion and love, dropping any outward personas that are no longer useful.

The flower essences star tulip and lotus may be helpful at this time to open up to deep guidance. Each person may share a song or poem that expresses Piscean feelings.

If you are alone, use paints or some other medium to convey your dreams. Read poetry such as the poems of William Blake, which have a strong mystical quality. Listen to music like Paul Horn's *Inside the Great Pyramid*, Indian ragas, Georgia Kelly's tapes like *Ancient Echoes*, or Paul Winter's *Canyon Consort*. Meditate and attune to the cosmic messages coming to you at this time.

Equinox and Solstice Ceremonies

Ceremonies and rituals are conducted by many groups at the time of the Sun's entry into the four cardinal signs: Aries and Libra, Spring and Fall Equinox, when days and nights are equal; and Cancer and Capricorn, Summer and Winter Solstice, times of the longest and shortest days.

Many groups also conduct ceremonies at cross-quarter days, which, along with the equinox and solstice times, are the eight Sabbats in the Wiccan tradition. At the following times we experience the manifestation of the energy begun at the equinoxes and solstices: February 2—Brigid's Day or Candlemas; May 1—Beltane or May Day, one of the ancient fire festivals; August 1—Lughnasadh or Lammas; and October 31—Samhain or Hallowe'en, another of the ancient fire festivals in Europe.

It is important to choose a sacred area or place of power for rituals. When possible, an outdoor spot is preferable, as natural elements—creeks, rocks, and trees, as well as birds and animals that might be present—make a strong contribution to the ceremony. Places where rituals have been done previously retain those vibrations, as do many spots that have been sacred to cultures that have inhabited the land, as is true of many Native American ceremonial places on this continent. It is also good to do rituals in different spots on various peoples' land so that the Earth may experience the healing energy all over.

A central focus in all ceremonies is the *fire*. Use of ritual fires derives from the sacred fire festivals in Europe (see James G. Frazer's *Golden Bough*, Macmillan, 1960) and the veneration of Grandfather Fire by all primitive peoples. Fire imitates the action of the Sun in its light and warmth. Ancient peoples would naturally tend to use fire at the Summer and Winter solstices, the two points of the year when the fire and heat of the Sun begin to wax and to wane, respectively.

Fire is also symbolic of purification, a strong element in all the ancient fire festivals where fire was used to purge plague and pestilence as well as individual spiritual demons. Native Americans use the sweat lodge as a way of bodily and spiritual purification and as preparation prior to ceremonies.

Form of Rituals

The night preceding the ceremony, women and men may split up, each group conducting its own special rituals before regrouping at dawn.

It is common for women to do Moon ceremonies honoring Grandmother Moon and the various Moon goddesses (Diana, Artemis, Astarte, Ishtar). Chants and songs may be sung to invoke the creative, fertile, and intuitive nature of the Moon. Crystals may be used and planted in the ground at various power spots. A Moon altar may be built around the sacred fire where women can place their special power objects and jewelry to be blessed by the light of the Moon. (These objects can be retrieved after dawn ceremonies.)

A medicine bundle may also be made and passed to every woman so that each can place a sacred object in the bundle. This bundle can then be used throughout the year by anyone in the circle when she is in need of special healing—physical, emotional, or spiritual.

Chants and songs can be shared, as can any important dreams or messages for the season of the year.

Chant to Honor Grandmother Moon

Into the silence of the night,
Into the silence of the Moon,
I am making my dreams come true.
Into the silence of the night,
Into the silence of the Moon,
I am making my being come true.
> (from *Medicine Wheel Chants*, Bear Tribe Medicine Society,
> P. O. Box 9167, Spokane, WA 99209)

Neesa, Neesa, Neesa,
Neesa, Neesa, Neesa,
Neesa, Neesa, Neesa,
Gay-we-o, Gay-we-o.

(from Brooke Medicine Eagle's *A Gift of Song,* available through Harmony Network, P. O. Box 9725, Berkeley, CA 94709)

Men can also make a circle with their power objects and the creation of a special medicine bundle. Often men conduct a sweat lodge at night for purification prior to the dawn ceremonies. The lodge itself may be built the day prior unless there is an already existing lodge. It is important to receive correct instruction in building the lodge with willow branches and in heating the rocks and stones.

At dawn, men and women may come together and share prayers around a sacred fire or in a sacred circle. The Native American custom is to hand a pinch of tobacco to each person and have each one in turn approach the sacred fire, making prayers and throwing the tobacco into the fire. Before this is done, someone comes around with burning sage, cedar, or sweetgrass and "smudges" each person. This is a way of purifying the aura of each individual in the ceremony and casting out any negative vibrations that may be around. Often people make little bundles ahead of time with a pinch of tobacco wrapped in red cloth. This is done for individuals who cannot be present. These tobacco bundles are placed in the fire after the individual makes a prayer. After the prayers, there may be sharing of chants, stories, music, and dreams. At the end, there is the breaking of the fast (for some this may have been just overnight; for others it may have been four days) and a feast to celebrate the new season and new energy.

The sacred fire or ceremonial altar is usually decorated with special plants and herbs of the season as well as colors and symbols for the four directions. East represents air. It symbolizes light, generation, and the color yellow; a feather or a representation of the eagle may be placed in the East. South is fire, a place of open heartedness and innocence; its color is red. Some fire symbol, or the mouse, the animal representative of this direction, may be placed there. West is water. It is a place of death and transformation; its color is black. A bowl of water may be placed in the West along with the black bear. North is earth, a place of wisdom and purification; its color is white. Place cornmeal to represent Earth and the white buffalo to symbolize the North.

WINTER SOLSTICE

Winter is the beginning of the cycle—the birth of the Sun King who brings back the light and leads us out of darkness. As the shortest day passes, the days increase in light, and we look within ourselves to find that new source of light and regeneration. In the Christian tradition, this is the time of the birth of Christ from Mary's womb; it is also the time of the birth of the Goddess and the time when Persephone returns from the underground and is reunited with her mother Demeter.

Native American tribes celebrate Earth Renewal ceremonies during the Winter Solstice. This is a time for fasting (usually for four days), purification, and staying close to Nature, avoiding cars and business in the outside world. It is also a time when medicine bundles of each clan or society are opened and renewed. North is the direction associated with winter. Its animal symbol is the white buffalo; often stories of White Buffalo Woman were told in Native American circles.

Winter solstice ceremonies were small compared with the large gatherings at midsummer. In Europe, the custom of the yule log was done at this time. The yule log, the counterpart of the midsummer bonfires, was kindled indoors instead of out in the open air due to the inclement weather of the season. In parts of Serbia today and in the Slavic nations, the yule log is still brought in and placed on the floor of the hearth where it glows underneath the fire for the twelve nights of the holiday season. After that, it is kept in the house all year to protect the home and inhabitants from adverse weather conditions and illness.

The sacred plant at this time of year is mistletoe. Mistletoe was worshipped by the Druids, the priests of the old Celts. It grew on the oak tree, which was sacred to the Druidic religion. Mistletoe had a variety of uses, from being a cure for epilepsy to helping women conceive. It was customary to place this plant around the midwinter fire.

The night before Winter Solstice is the darkest night, symbolic of the gestation in the womb before birth. Rituals may be done where each person in the circle lies in a womblike state and one woman, impersonating the Goddess, touches each person, bringing them to birth. As all rise and become born, they may ask for what they want to manifest in this new cycle and offer any prayers they have for the Earth and the planet at this time. Meditations may be done to focus the light on specific areas of consciousness.

Earth Renewal rituals are often performed the following morning. Such a ritual follows:

At dawn, the oldest woman, the oldest man, the youngest maiden of consciousness, and the youngest man of consciousness gather in a circle with the sacred fire at the center. The oldest woman and maiden stand in the West. The oldest man stands in the East; the young man enters from the North.

The oldest woman moves clockwise inside the circle and digs a hole with a crystal; she places corn seeds in the hole and prays for the seeds to be fulfilled. Next the maiden enters and sprinkles pollen on the seeds, praying for the unborn. Meanwhile, the youngest boy has started his run for the Sun, carrying water in his mouth. He tries to time it so that he enters the circle from the East as the maiden is leaving the gateway. If he arrives too soon, he runs around the outside of the circle. As he goes around the fire Sun-wise, he lets the water out of his mouth onto the seeds and pollen, offering a prayer for rain. He leaves the circle and returns to a place in the circle near the oldest man in the East. The oldest man enters and covers the seeds, offering prayers in remembrance of our finite nature. He returns to his place, moving Sun-wise around the circle.

After this ritual is completed, one person may hand a pinch of tobacco to all present, and each one makes individual prayers around the fire. Chants and songs are then shared.

The following are two songs that are appropriate for this time of year.

Light is Returning

One planet is turning, circle on her path around the Sun
Earth Mother is calling her children home.
Light is returning, although this is the darkest hour
No one can hold back the dawn.
Let's keep it burning, let's keep the light of hope alive,
Make safe the journey, through the storm.

by Charlie Murphy (from the tape *Canticles of Light*, produced by Art Front Music, P. O. Box 12188, Seattle, WA 98102)

Ancient Mother

Ancient Mother, I hear you calling
Ancient Mother, I hear your sound
Ancient Mother, I hear your laughter
Ancient Mother, I taste your tears.

SPRING EQUINOX

As the day force and the night force become equal, the Earth renews her cycle of birth and resurrection. Plants buried underground during the long winter months raise their heads, leaves appear on the trees, the buzz of insects fills the air, and the bright colors of spring flowers dominate the landscape. This is the time when Demeter and Persephone, mother and daughter, play together on the Earth amongst the purples and yellows of spring growth. It is a time to begin again, to plant seeds in our gardens and seeds for our own growth process during the new cycle. What is it that is important for each of us to accomplish in the next cycle, and how can we initiate that action at this time?

For our rituals, we can hang sprigs of fresh herbs and flowers of yellow, orange, and purple on our altars and in our sacred circles. As we place our crystals, we can emphasize those of yellow and orange hues, like citrine and topaz, that symbolize the return of the Sun. Other power objects might include feathers of birds that are special to us, parts of animals, shells, rocks, and minerals.

East is the direction associated with spring, the color red, the eagle, dawn, and new beginnings. The egg is also a symbol of spring; the Easter egg is a carry-over of the Goddess' egg that was opened by a serpent. The egg represents birth and hatching.

Chants can be sung to celebrate the rebirth of Nature's kingdom. Here are some good chants for the spring:

Spirit of the Wind

chorus
Spirit of the wind, carry me
Spirit of the wind, carry me home
Spirit of the wind, carry me home to myself.
Spirit of the ocean, depth of emotion
Spirit of the sea, set my soul free.
Spirit of the storm, help me be reborn
Spirit of the rain, wash away my pain.
Spirit of the Sun, warm light healing me
Spirit of the sky, spread my wings and fly.
Spirit of the river, blessed forgiver
Spirit of the shore, show me more and more.
Spirit of the Earth, help me with my birth
Spirit of the land, hold me in your hand.

The Return

The earth, the water, the fire, the air
Return, return, return, return
The earth, the water, the fire, the air
Return, return, return, return.
Ee ya ya ya ya ya ya ya
Wo wo wo wo wo wo wo wo
Ee ya ya ya ya ya ya ya
Wo wo wo wo wo wo wo wo.

SUMMER SOLSTICE

As the light of the Sun increases, we approach the time of the Summer Solstice, or Midsummer's Eve. This is the longest day of the year; in European societies it was traditional to celebrate all night with open fires, songs, dancing, mead, and ale. This is a time to unleash the dark forces within us, to celebrate with each other and prepare for the waning of the Sun's power.

One European custom was to roll a burning wheel down a hillside to imitate the action of the Sun at this time. (There was also the idea that this would purify any evil spirits around.)

Just as the mistletoe is associated with the Winter Solstice, St. John's Wort is the sacred herb of summer. (St. John's Day is usually celebrated on June 24.) St. John's Wort is a strong healing herb and has many psychic properties; it is often placed under the pillow to enhance dreams. From St. John's Wort comes a deep red oil that is helpful for cuts, bruises, insect bites, and other wounds.

St. John's Wort is often placed around the sacred fire or altar. Since yellow is the color of summer, brilliant summer flowers and plants and yellow objects adorn our ritual space. The mouse is the animal symbolic of this season, suggesting innocence and intuition.

In the Demeter-Persephone myth, Persephone comes of age at Beltane (May Day) and on Summer Solstice enters the labyrinth that takes her underground to the realms of Hecate. The descent into the underground is begun as the power of the Sun wanes.

Rituals at this time celebrate the fertility and abundance of the Earth with a seed of preparation for the darkness that lies ahead. After meditations and attunements, rituals should include a lot of singing and dancing to commemorate this time. A spiral dance symbolizing Persephone's descent into the underworld can also be done.

The Earth Is Our Mother
(adaptation of a Hopi chant)
The Earth is our Mother,
We must take care of her.
The Earth is our Mother,
We must take care of her.
Hey yunga yo yunga hey yung yung
Hey yunga yo yunga hey yung yung
Her sacred ground we walk upon
With every step we take.
Her sacred ground we walk upon
With every step we take.
Hey yunga yo yunga hey yung yung

I Circle Around
(from an Arapaho Ghost Dance song)
I circle around, I circle around
The boundaries of the Earth.
I circle around, I circle around
The boundaries of the Earth.
Wearing my long-winged feathers as I fly,
Wearing my long-winged feathers as I fly,
I circle around, I circle around
The boundaries of the Earth.

FALL EQUINOX
The time of equal day and night marks the beginning of the death of the Sun King and the time to gather the harvest and reap what we have sown at the Spring Equinox. Our sacred circles are surrounded with sheaves of corn, pine cones, squashes, pumpkins, and other fall foods and plants. The harvest abundance is present, but so is the sense of preparation and storing for the dark cold winter and the death of Nature. Fall Equinox is the time Demeter mourns for Persephone, or in the other mythological cycles (as the Ishtar and Tammuz cycle), the Goddess mourns for her consort. It is a time of going within ourselves and making preparations for how we will survive, physically and spiritually, during the winter months. Fall is symbolized by the West, the black bear, the middle years of our life when we go within to seek that wisdom and knowledge that is equated with winter and old age.

This is a time to gather supplies (shells, feathers, seed pods) for winter crafts like basket making and jewelry.

In the ritual for fall, it is important for all to give up something they are letting go of in their lives, some emotion or habit pattern that they want to die at this time. After all have shared what this is, each makes prayers of gratitude for something received from the harvest of Earth's bounty.

Here is a chant for fall:

Changing Woman
She changes everything she touches,
And everything she touches, changes.
Changing woman, rearranges,
Changing woman, rearranges.

CROSS-QUARTER DAYS

There are four other times of the year when it is customary among certain groups to conduct rituals. These times, midway between the solstices and equinoxes, were celebrated by the ancient Celts. Many festivals are still celebrated throughout Europe on these days. At these times, the energy inaugurated at the equinox and solstice points becomes manifest. The four days are October 31, Samhain or Hallowe'en; February 2, Brigid's Day or Candlemas; May 1, Beltane or May Day; and August 1, Lughnasadh or Lammas.

Samhain, or Hallowe'en

October 31 ends the year, and November 1 begins the new cycle. This is the transition from autumn to winter. It is the time when the Sun is in Scorpio, sign of death and transformation. At this time, the souls of the departed were supposed to visit their former homes and warm themselves by the fire. Now the veil is very thin between the world of humans and the realm of the goddesses and gods. This is because on Samhain, time belongs neither to the old year nor to the new but is in transition. Now is when the goddesses, gods, and departed souls can easily cross over. Bonfires blaze all over, and legend says that witches and fairies roam. In ancient Ireland, a new fire was kindled every year at this time, and from this sacred flame all the fires in Ireland were rekindled.

Since the veil between all creatures is lowered during Samhain, many animal spirits are present and speak through the witches at this time. The custom of costumes arose to impersonate these animal spirits and the spirits of the dead, to bring them back to life. This is a strong time for purification, for letting go of any "dead" issues, and for preparing for the New Year.

Individuals may now lay out their crystals and special power objects, especially any items that belonged to those recently departed. Prayers may be made for departed ones and for the new cycle. Animal spirits may be invoked for their protection and powers. Many tribal societies invoke the spirits of departed ancestors at Hallowe'en. This is a good time for using crystal balls for scrying and looking into the next cycle.

All Hallows represents the underworld or labyrinth in the Demeter-Persephone myth. This was the time when Demeter descended into the labyrinth in search of Persephone.

For the Samhain ritual, a circular place is needed, with a central fire or cauldron with coals. People form a circle and begin a spiral dance, counterclockwise moving into the center of the labyrinth. This is generally done in silence. At a certain time, the spiral becomes a circle again. All put something into the fire that they want to banish or get rid of. This can be done verbally or silently or can be written on pieces of paper that are then thrown into the fire. Then, all sit down and do a meditation or attunement to the spirit world and the beginning of the new cycle. Afterwards, the spiral dance is repeated, but this time the movement is clockwise, from death to rebirth, from darkness into light.

She's Been Waiting
She's been waiting, waiting, she's been waiting so long,
She's been waiting for her children to remember to return.
Blessed be and blessed are the lovers of the lady,
Blessed be and blessed are the Mother, Maid, and Crone.
Blessed be and blessed are the ones who dance together,
Blessed be and blessed are the ones who dance alone.

Who Were the Witches?
(chorus)
Who were the witches?
Where did they come from?
Maybe your great-great-grandmother was one.
Witches were wise, wise women they say,
And there's a little witch in every woman today.
Witches knew all about flowers and weeds

How to use all their roots and their seeds.
When people grew weary from hard-working days,
They made them feel better in so many ways.
When women had babies, the witches were there,
To help them and hold them and give them sweet care.
Witches knew stories about how life began,
Do you wish you could be one? Well, maybe you can.
Some people thought that the witches were bad,
Some people feared all the power they had.
But the power to help and to heal and to cure
Is nothing to fear, it is something to share.

Brigid's Day, or Candlemas

This is a time of celebrating the increasing light born at the Winter Solstice. Since it is the time of Aquarius, it is when we celebrate our contributions toward humanity.

On Candlemas, winter begins to give way to spring. Persephone is returned from the underworld. This is the time of the feast of poets, the nine muses. It is the time in Wicca when priestesses are initiated into the Coven and dedicate themselves to the Goddess. Any rituals done at this time should emphasize the creative contributions of each person present. People may bring poems, songs, art projects, and other work to share.

Rituals for Candlemas begin with some kind of purification, the cleansing away of the dark force and winter. Sage or sweetgrass, salt water, or various types of incense may be used. After some type of attunement, each person shares something creative, symbolizing the beginnings of longer days and the movement toward spring and the generative force.

Giveaway

Our magic is our giveaway,
Our magic is our song,
So give away your love today,
And sing the whole day long.

Beltane, or May Day

This festival derives from the ancient fire festivals of Europe, as does Samhain. It was probably dedicated to the Celtic god Belenus, although little is known of him. May Day celebrates the springtime and Mother Earth's fertility. It is the time of Taurus. At this time, the cattle were taken to their summer grazing spots and driven through purificatory fires by the Druid priests, and fertility rites to the Mother Goddess were performed. In some places, people danced naked in the fields to assure the fertility of the grain. During the day, they danced around the Maypole; at night, there were fire rituals and leaping over bonfires.

In the mythological cycles of Ishtar-Tammuz and Isis-Osiris, May is the time of the sacred marriage; it is also the time of Demeter and Persephone's reunion.

Modern May Day rituals work with the Earth's fertility and procreative powers. Thanks may be given for the abundance of spring herbs and flowers. Ceremonies may also be performed to bless individual plants for their healing powers.

Place a pole in the center with decorative streamers, along with flower wreaths that participants have woven. Off to the side, have a fire pit where a sacred fire is started at the beginning of the ceremony. This is a fire of love, and when jumping over it, individuals may release into the fire any old programs or strictures in their love relationships. Later in the evening, the fire may be jumped over a second time, and this time new openings of the heart are requested.

Blessings of the Goddess

May the blessings of the Goddess rest upon you.
May her peace abide in you.
May her presence illuminate your heart.
Now and forever more.

The River

The river she is flowing,
Flowing and growing
The river she is flowing,
Down to the sea.
Mother, carry me,
A child I will always be
Mother, carry me,
A child I will always be.

Lughnasadh, or Lammas

August 1, Lughnasadh, was a festival sacred to the Celtic god Lugus, which marked the harvest. (Lammas was the Christian name given to this festival.) The blooming of the Earth has not yet stopped, but there is a strong transition about to take place. Persephone has left Demeter and entered the labyrinth leading to the underworld.

We can create many ceremonies at this time to celebrate the Sun's power and to concentrate on opening our hearts to the love and gifts of the Earth Mother. Corn is an important element in these ceremonies; often the altar or ceremonial center is decorated with corn sheaves, fruit such as grapes, and other grains. A bowl of cornmeal is also on the altar or around the sacred fire. In the rituals performed, all can tune in to the coming harvest and ask for what they want to harvest in their own life. After giving thanks to the Earth Mother, corn bread is often eaten, showing the change of the grain into bread; wine is often shared as well, symbolizing the transformation of the grapes into wine. This begins a season of change, just as we often perceive a touch of fall in August mornings.

Give Thanks

Give thanks to the Mother Gaia,
Give thanks to the Father Sun,
Give thanks to the beautiful garden,
Where the Mother and Father are one.
Give thanks, give thanks, to you we do give thanks,
Give thanks, give thanks, to you we do give thanks.

Case Histories Using Earth Mother Techniques

In order to understand how Holistic Astrology works with the various healing modalities, I am including several horoscopes, an analysis of each one, information on the case history of each client, and which of these tools the client has chosen to utilize.

Case History #1

The first horoscope (Natal Chart 1) shows a full seventh house and Virgo emphasis. The native is a male psychotherapist with a deep knowledge of physical therapies (nutrition and herbs) and astrology. Mutable emphasis is strong, with six planets in mutable signs (five of them are Mercury-ruled) along with the nodes. The Moon in the tenth in Sagittarius forms the handle in this general bucket formation. (All other planets are in the signs Gemini through Libra.)

Sun conjunct Neptune shows the potential for low blood sugar and allergies. With Uranus and Saturn in Gemini as well as the Moon in Sagittarius, the tendency might be toward respiratory allergies and lung ailments. The conglomeration of planets in the seventh house (the Libran house) could indicate a sensitivity to kidney problems. In addition, Saturn is square Venus, pointing again to the kidneys and possible skin problems. The Aquarius Ascendant, Mercury square Jupiter, and five Mercury-ruled planets show the need to balance and strengthen the nervous system.

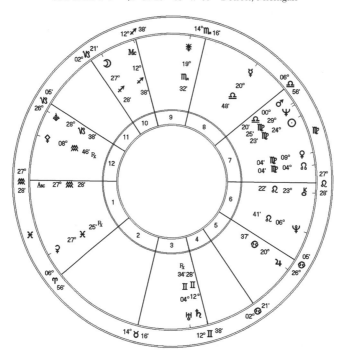

The client's health history included a kidney inflammation in 1965, for which penicillin was prescribed, and two years (1966–1968) of *Candida albicans*, for which he used Nystatin and later Nizerol (a fungal antibiotic). In addition, the client had weekly acupuncture treatments, used homeopathic remedies, and paid fairly close attention to his diet.

Based on his horoscope and confirmation through radiesthesia, the following supplements were recommended:

1. Magnesium (through taking liquid chlorophyll and also through potassium-magnesium capsules, potassium being important for the kidneys)

2. Manganese for the nervous system

3. Pantothenic acid for stress, allergies, and the tendency to hypoglycemia

4. Bioflavonoids for the kidneys and for allergies (Bioflavonoids are preferable to vitamin C since vitamin C is very acidic to the body.)

5. Vitamin A in the form of carrot juice or betaine hydrochloride tablets

6. Free-form amino acid capsules for general energy and low blood sugar

7. Zinc for the immune system

Specific herbs recommended were dandelion root and chicory for toning the liver and pancreas; cleavers, nettles, and uva ursi for the kidneys; and fennel, dill, and papaya leaf for aiding digestion.

In general, the dietary recommendation was for a strongly alkaline diet with an emphasis on whole grains, cooked vegetables, sea vegetables, and proteins. (Little mucus-forming proteins like meats and dairy, but some yogurt and lactic acid proteins, fish, tofu, and eggs were found to be beneficial.)

Flower remedies included beech for intolerance and being too critical of the self; pine for self-reproach and guilt; dill to help assimilate and digest experiences; and corn for finding one's balance between the outer social world (Virgo and Aquarius) and the inner psychic world (Neptune conjunct the Sun). Also recommended were cerato for doubting one's own abilities (Sun square Moon); agrimony for inner self-acceptance; penstemon for withdrawing from relationships (Saturn square Venus); sweet pea for group social relationships; and red clover for working with individual versus group egos as well as for personal cleansing and purifying.

In terms of colors, the reds and oranges seemed important to bring out the fire and increase physical vitality and stamina (Sun square Moon and mutable emphasis). The crystals topaz and citrine quartz were suggested to break up blockages in the solar plexus and increase personal power.

Among the aromatic oils, chamomile, marjoram, and rosemary were chosen to balance the nervous system (with five Mercury-ruled planets), as well as cardamom, fennel, hyssop, and thyme for digestion.

I first saw this client in November 1986; he had a kidney stone at the time. Saturn was square his natal Venus and about to conjoin his MC. The previous month's two eclipses were 135 degrees from his Ascendant, 135 degrees from Venus, opposite Mercury, and square Jupiter. His kidney stone had been diagnosed the previous August when he had pains in his back and ureter. He was torn between treating the condition with natural remedies and allowing the stone to pass on its own accord or having surgery. The stone was quite sizable and was located in a difficult place.

In our first consultation, we discussed supplements, diet, and herbs as well as the congestion and blockage of emotions from childhood (Saturn square Venus) that had led to the formation of the stone. With transiting Uranus square his natal Sun and Neptune, it seemed a good time period to let go of the old crystallizations.

In the second session, we began some deep emotional work, using relaxation techniques to enter a heightened state of awareness. In this state, the patient got in touch with many old scenes and traumas that were related to his physical symptoms. He began to relax his body further and to send healing to the particular area of the kidneys. A flower remedy was made of mimulus—for his fears related to passing the stone—and penstemon—for working in groups and emotional relationships. As the deep sessions continued, his higher self advised an emerald remedy (to which was added green garnet) and rosemary oil aromatically and in the bath.

An X-ray on December 1 revealed that the stone had moved four to five inches to the bladder area. Several deep sessions were done to empower him to pass the stone himself. He spent a weekend fasting and using olive oil and lemon juice to help pass the stone. It apparently was too large.

On January 14, 1987, the client underwent surgery while Uranus was exactly square his Sun. Six and one-half hours of surgery were required to remove the stone in many pieces. He suffered a lot of trauma and pain in the hospital. He had an internal catheter for three weeks to permit the uric acid to bypass the place where the kidney stone had been removed.

After the surgery, I recommended a homeopathic magnesium phosphate and lots of liquid chlorophyll, in addition to his regular supplements. He also benefited from flower remedies of chamomile for relaxation and chestnut bud for breaking old patterns.

In February, as he regained his health and vitality, the flower remedy lotus was used for transformation and advancement on his spiritual path.

A few months later, the client's own therapy practice expanded greatly, and the size of the therapeutic men's groups he had been leading more than doubled. His physical energy and vitality continue to be very strong, and he still works with his diet, herbal and homeopathic remedies, and flower remedies when necessary.

Case History #2

The second horoscope (Natal Chart 2) shows the 1936 opposition of Saturn in Pisces to Neptune in Virgo broadly squared by Jupiter, indicating the tendency to hypoglycemia, allergies, and conditions relating to immune system deficiency. Jupiter square Venus also points up blood sugar problems. With the Sun conjunct Mercury, an Aquarius Ascendant, and Mars conjunct Uranus, this woman has a highly sensitive nervous system and will need a lot of grounding. The Moon at 29 degrees Scorpio, close to the Midheaven, receives a 22-1/2 degree aspect from Mars. This shows strong emotional issues and the need to balance the reproductive and hormonal systems. The grand trine from the Moon to Venus and Pluto is helpful, as is the Moon's conjunction to Ceres, emphasizing a nurturing warm nature and the ability to heal any hormonal imbalances.

This woman has been diagnosed as immune deficient, manifesting chronic Epstein-Barr virus (a mono-like virus that causes extreme fatigue, depression, digestive disorders, and various low-grade infections).

NATAL CHART 2 (Koch Houses) • FEMALE April 10, 1936
3:19 AM PST • 37° N 52´ 122°W 16´ Oakland, California

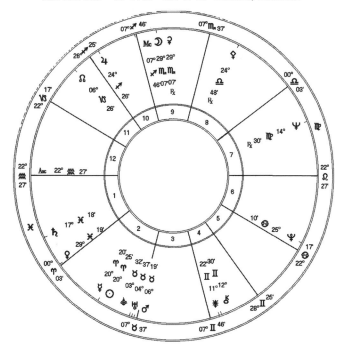

179

With this horoscope, there should be a strong emphasis on vitamins and minerals for the nervous and immune systems. The following supplements would be appropriate:

1. Magnesium, particularly from liquid chlorophyll, as well as a potassium-magnesium or calcium-magnesium capsule

2. Manganese for the nervous system

3. Pantothenic acid for stress and allergies

4. Vitamin B-12 for the nervous system and to aid assimilation of iron (Saturn and Venus in Pisces)

5. Bioflavonoids for allergies and general health maintenance

6. Vitamin E for hormonal balance

7. Flax seed oil or evening primrose oil (both contain prostaglandins) for hormonal balance

8. Free-form amino acid capsules for blood sugar and general energy

9. Zinc for the immune system

10. An adrenal glandular supplement

Particular herbs that would be helpful are those that stimulate the adrenal glands (Sun and Mercury in Aries), such as gotu kola and fo ti (Chinese herb of longevity); herbs to tone the liver and pancreas, like dandelion root and chicory; herbs for the immune system, including chaparral, echinacea root, and the Chinese herb astragalus; and herbs for hormonal balance, like dong quai, squawvine, and raspberry leaf.

Several flower remedies would be beneficial over the course of therapy: for the Aries Sun and Mercury, impatiens to relax tensions and develop patience, and heather to balance out the Arian self-centeredness. A Scorpio Moon indicates the need for willow to release old resentments, holly to transform hatred and jealousy, sticky monkeyflower to balance out sexual energy and break free of repressions, and garlic for debilitating fears and insecurities. An Aquarius Ascendant suggests the need for walnut to break links with the past and leave behind old patterns, vervain for extremes of mental energy that manifest as stress and tension, and chamomile to help the nervous system.

Aromatic essences appropriate for this woman include basil, ginger, and black pepper for stimulation to the adrenals and enhancing basic vitality, and chamomile, rosemary, and marjoram to relax the nervous system. Colors of blue and blue-greens would be soothing to the nervous system, and at certain times, reds and oranges would be useful in elevating the vital energy.

Working with crystals such as smoky quartz and black obsidian can bring out the positive regenerative qualities of the Scorpio Moon—seeing the light in the dark and transforming the dark forces. Lapis lazuli and sapphire are good stones to wear to balance Uranian energy, and rose quartz is a fine crystal to work with Venus in Pisces.

I first saw this client in March 1987. She had been ill for three years and out of work since July 1984, when she had been taken to a hospital emergency room with spasms of the esophagus. Subsequent tests revealed a lactose intolerance. After much frustration and difficulty with the medical establishment, she found some holistically-oriented physicians who diagnosed her as having *Candida albicans* (a yeast-like fungus that causes sensitivity to foods, hair loss, fatigue, and emotional depression) and Epstein-Barr syndrome. She was placed on a restricted diet and given many nutritional supplements. She had been losing weight over this three-year period, and her doctor wanted to put her in the hospital for a gamma globulin infusion to boost her immune system. He also wanted to administer small amounts of Cortisol, a cortisone drug for the immune system. Since she had a tendency to be allergic to medications, she did not want either of these treatments.

After making a careful analysis of her diet, supplements, and herbs, we began some deep emotional therapy where many of her latent fears came out. As a child, she had a fear of leaving home and sleeping away from home. Her parents were extremely protective of her and her sister. She had many fears regarding physical activities. She always felt different from other children and did not enjoy the usual parties and activities during her school years. From 1950–1954 during high school, she had eczema over her body, some hair loss, and allergies.

In addition to our sessions, I referred her to a chiropractic doctor who uses applied kinesiology to determine structural, nutritional, biochemical, and emotional imbalances. He did cranial work with her to balance the nervous system, and neuro-vascular dynamics work for deep organ regeneration. Later, she had some acupuncture sessions.

The first flower remedy she had during our sessions included walnut for her oversensitivity to outside ideas and parental influences, mimulus for her fears, and Indian paintbrush to work with her vital energy. She also bought some crystals, particularly rose quartz and amethyst. Her energy continued vascillating from low at times to good at other times. We worked with her dreams, through which many of her fears were expressed, and also explored some past lives to find the source of her qualms and blockages. As her energy improved, she took some yoga classes and began to incorporate yoga into her daily schedule.

During the next few months, I gave her the following flower remedies: pomegranate to access her feminine creative energy, hornbeam for mental and physical exhaustion, and wild rose for enthusiasm and energy. She reinforced the flower remedies with affirmations.

We continued working on empowering her so she could design her own healing program and not be influenced by medical professionals who continually wanted to give her cortisone drugs. She has now expanded her diet to include other foods that had been prohibited under the *Candida* diet. She also learned to use a pendulum so she could check herself for various foods, herbs, and supplements. She has not yet returned to any regular work schedule. When she does, she has decided that it will be quite a different career from her previous work in banking.

Case History #3

The third horoscope (Natal Chart 3) shows a preponderance in fire signs, with five Leo planets, an Aries Moon, and a Sagittarian Saturn and Ascendant. With the water houses emphasized, an angular Moon and Cancer Sun, emotional and psychic sensitivity is strong. The grand fire trines with Uranus, Mercury, and Mars indicate a spiritual and creative nature. In fact, the native started doing some spiritual channeling when he was 18.

Mercury conjunct Uranus and Mars indicates a highly charged nervous system, new innovative ideas, and a lot of running around. With all his fire, including a Sagittarian Ascendant, this individual tends to "burn himself out" and needs to build up his adrenal energy. Mars is also square the nodes, signifying a very emotional nature and, with the Aries Moon, probably a good deal of anger. Jupiter in Virgo is the only real earth element in the horoscope; it squares the Ascendant, which could indicate some problems with the pancreas and liver. Saturn in Sagittarius indicates potential problems with the lungs and respiratory system; this is also shown by the Mercury-Uranus conjunction.

NATAL CHART 3 (Koch Houses) • MALE July 18, 1957
4:59 PM CST • 31° N 18´ 92° W 27´ Alexandria, Louisiana

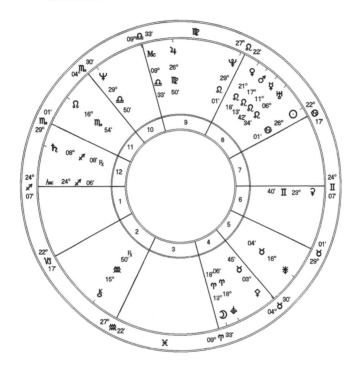

This man has been addicted to alcohol and has also used many types of drugs throughout his life. He had a difficult childhood with a mother who was an abusive alcoholic. His parents were separated, and he spent several years of his childhood moving up and down the East Coast with his father, sisters, and brother before coming back to California to live with his mother again. Throughout his life he has been subject to depression and hypoglycemia.

Based on his horoscope and history, the following nutritional supplements were recommended and confirmed by the use of radiesthesia.

1. Liquid chlorophyll to help detoxify his liver and provide magnesium

2. 2 T olive oil and 1/2 of a fresh lemon a couple times a week to cleanse the liver and gallbladder

3. Psyllium seed husks and aloe vera juice alternate mornings for cleansing the colon

4. Free-form amino acid tablets to balance the blood sugar and to give energy

5. Manganese tablets for his nervous system

6. Pantothenic acid to alleviate stress and to stimulate the adrenal cortex in keeping up energy and blood sugar

7. Zinc for the immune system

8. A pancreas glandular supplement

9. Bioflavonoid capsules for the lungs and general health

10. Octacosanol to bring more oxygen to his lungs

Recommended herbs included Oregon grape root and dandelion root for the liver, gallbladder, and pancreas; mullein, coltsfoot, and comfrey for the lungs; marshmallow root for both the respiratory system and adrenals; and gotu kola and fo ti for the adrenals.

Flower remedies that seemed appropriate for this individual through studying his horoscope and life circumstances were:

1. Honeysuckle—for letting go of past feelings and emotions

2. Larch—for lack of confidence and anticipation of failure

3. Golden eardrops—to release childhood memories and early emotional experiences

4. Mariposa lily—for trauma in parent-child bonding and for feeling unloved

5. Yarrow—for psychic protection and protection against environmental influence

6. Clematis—for indifference, dreaminess, lack of concentration, and impracticality

7. Manzanita—for grounding, balancing, and opening up to higher consciousness

8. Vine—to bring out leadership qualities of the Leo planets

9. Borage—to bring lightness and humor

10. Wild oat—to focus on ambitions while dispelling feelings of dissatisfaction and despondency

Various aromatic essences were also helpful in bringing about this client's emotional and spiritual balance. Recommended aromas included melissa for its uplifting quality and its strengthening of the nerves and brain, clary sage for depression and as a tonic for the nerves, frankincense for soothing the mind and emotions, and myrrh for strengthening the pulmonary system.

The colors indigo, violet, and purple bring in a higher vibration. In terms of stones and crystals, turquoise relates to the liver, increasing the bile flow and promoting cleansing. The crystals amethyst and fluorite enable the mind to maintain a meditative state in the midst of activity. With his strong eighth house, smoky quartz was important for seeing the light in dark areas and for transcending and altering the darkness.

I first saw this man in April 1986 at the time of his Saturn return. He was doing physical work and some crystal mining, which brought him much happiness. He was very shy and sensitive and had difficulties with groups of people. He also had a lot of anger—toward his mother, particularly, and toward his ex-wife, with whom his two children lived. He had problems with her in arranging to see his children.

He wanted to cleanse his body and get help with nutritional supplements and diet. He mentioned that he used to drink quite a bit and had used many recreational drugs in the past. We worked with a more alkaline diet stressing whole grains, especially in the morning, to keep his blood sugar steady; lots of cooked vegetables; and nonmucus-forming proteins. We also recommended herbs and supplements helpful in balancing his body, and cleansing treatments, including colonics.

As we began to work in deeper sessions, he used the following flower remedies: clematis, yarrow, honeysuckle, mariposa lily, and wild oat. He also utilized vervain for his tendency to worry and his high-strung nervous system. He was mining crystals and using them to heal himself.

It wasn't until Uranus hit his Ascendant by transit that he was able to openly admit his alcohol problem. In November 1986 he joined AA and went to regular meetings. He found that he was able to overcome some of his timidity in speaking with groups. He also began to travel more to sell crystals and to mine crystals in different parts of the United States.

He has not yet resolved his anger, especially toward his mother and ex-wife. He still uses alcohol when he gets depressed, but has continued to use nutritional supplements that help to balance his energy and control his blood sugar.

Bibliography

Chapter I In the Beginning—Elements, Qualities, Planets, Signs, and Houses

Forrest, Steven. *The Inner Sky*. San Diego, CA: ACS Publications, Inc., 1994.

George, Demetra. *Asteroid Goddesses*. San Diego, CA: ACS Publications, Inc., 1986.

Hand, Robert. *Horoscope Symbols*. Gloucester, MA: Para Research, Inc., 1981.

Moore, Marcia and Mark Douglas. *Astrology, the Divine Science*. York Harbor, ME: Arcane Publications, 1971.

Naiman, Ingrid. *The Astrology of Healing, Vol. II*. Santa Fe, NM: Ingrid Naiman, 1984.

Nauman, Eileen. *The American Book of Nutrition & Medical Astrology*. San Diego, CA: ACS Publications, Inc., 1982.

Oken, Alan. *Alan Oken's Complete Astrology*. New York, NY: Bantam Books, 1998.

Starck, Marcia. *Astrology: Key to Holistic Health*. Birmingham, MI: Seek-It Publications, 1982.

Chapter II Planetary Rulership over Vitamins and Minerals

Ballentine, Rudolph, M.D. *Diet and Nutrition: A Holistic Approach*. Honesdale, PA: Himalayan Publications, 1978.

Haas, Elson, M.D. *Staying Healthy with the Seasons*. Millbrae, CA: Celestial Arts, 1981.

_____. *Staying Healthy with Nutrition*. Millbrae, CA: Celestial Arts, 1992.

Heritage, Ford. *Composition and Facts about Foods*. Mokelumne Hill, CA: Health Research, 1971.

Rohe, Fred. *The Complete Book of Natural Foods*. Boulder, CO: Shambhala Publications, Inc., 1983.

Chapter III Herbs and Astrological Signs

Gladstar, Rosemary. *Herbal Healing for Women*. New York, NY: Simon & Schuster, 1993.

Grieve, M. *A Modern Herbal*. Mineola, NY: Dover Publications, Inc., 1971.

Hutchens, Alma R. *Indian Herbology of North America*. Windsor, Ontario: Merco, 1969.

Kloss, Jethro. *Back to Eden*. New York, NY: Benedict Lust Publications, 1971.

Lucas, Richard. *Secrets of the Chinese Herbalists*. New York: Cornerstone Library, Inc., 1979.

Lust, John. *The Herb Book*. New York, NY: Benedict Lust Publications, 1974.

Santillo, Humbart. *Natural Healing with Herbs*. Prescott Valley, AZ: Hohm Press, 1984.

Tierra, Lesley. *The Herbs of Life*. Freedom, CA: The Crossing Press, 1992.

Tierra, Michael. *The Way of Herbs*. Berkeley, CA: Orenda Publishing/Unity Press, 1980.

Chapter IV Planets and Signs and Their Relationship to Music and Color

Brennan, Barbara. *Hands of Light*. New York, NY: Bantam Books, 1987.

Berendt, Joachim. *The World is Sound: Nada Brahman*. Rochester, VT: Inner Traditions, 1991.

Clark, Linda. *The Ancient Art of Color Therapy*. New York, NY: Simon & Schuster, Inc., 1975.

David, William. *The Harmonics of Sound, Color & Vibration*. Marina del Rey, CA: De Vorss & Co., 1980.

Dinshah, Darius. *The Spectro-Chrome System*. Malaga, NJ: Dinshah Health Society, 1979.

Gardner-Gordon, Joy. *Color and Crystals*. Freedom, CA: The Crossing Press, 1988.

_____. *The Healing Voice*. Freedom, CA: The Crossing Press, 1993.

Gimbel, Theo. *Healing Through Colour*. Saffron Walden, Essex, Great Britain: C.W. Daniel Co., Ltd., 1980.

Heline, Corinne. *Healing & Regeneration Through Music*. Santa Barbara, CA: J.F. Rowny Press, 1968.

_____. *Healing & Regeneration Through Color*. Santa Barbara, CA: J.F. Rowny Press, 1972.

_____. *Color & Music in the New Age*. Marina del Rey, CA: De Vorss & Co., 1985.

Keyes, Laurel. *Toning: The Creative Power of the Voice*. Marina del Rey, CA: De Vorss & Co., 1964.

Lingerman, Hal. *The Healing Energies of Music*. Wheaton, IL: Theosophical Publishing House, 1983.

Tame, David. *The Secret Power of Music: The Transformation of Self & Society Through Musical Energy*. New York, NY: Destiny Books, 1984.

Chapter V Planetary Healing with Crystals and Gemstones

Baer, Randall & Vicki. *Windows of Light*. San Francisco, CA: Harper & Row Publishers, Inc., 1984.

Bhattacharya, Benoytosh. *Gem Therapy*. Calcutta: Firma KLM Private Limited, 1985.

Dow, Jane Ellen. *Crystal Journey: Travel Guide for the New Shaman*. Santa Fe, NM: Journey Books, 1994.

Isaacs, Thelma. *Gemstones, Crystals, & Healing*. Black Mountain, NC: Lorien House, 1982.

Lorusso, Julia & Joel Glick. *Healing Stoned: The Therapeutic Use of Gems & Minerals.* Albuquerque, NM: Adobe Press, 1976.

Mella, Dorothy. *Stone Power.* Albuquerque, NM: Brotherhood of Life, Inc., 1986.

Raphaell, Katrina. *Crystal Enlightenment: Vol. I.* New York: Aurora Press, 1985.

_____. *Crystal Healing: Vol. II.* New York: Aurora Press, 1987.

Uyldert, Mellie. *The Magic of Precious Stones.* Wellingborough, Northamptonshire, England: Turnstone Press, 1981.

Chapter VI Flower Remedies and Astrological Signs

Chancellor, Philip M. *Handbook of the Bach Flower Remedies.* London: C.W. Daniel Co. Ltd., 1971.

Cunningham, Donna. *Flower Remedies Handbook.* New York, NY: Sterling Publishing, 1991.

Harvey, Clare and Cochrane, Amanda. *The Encyclopedia of Flower Essences.* London: Thorsons, 1995.

Kaminski, Patricia and Katz, Richard. *Flower Essence Repertory.* Nevada City, CA: Flower Essence Society, 1996.

Small-Wright, Machaelle. *Flower Essences.* Jeffersonton, VA: Perelandra, Ltd., 1988.

Chapter VII Aromatherapy and Planetary Correspondences

Keville, Kathy and Green, Mindy. *Aromatheraphy: A Complete Guide to the Healing Art.* Freedom, CA: The Crossing Press, 1995.

Price, Shirley. *Practical Aromatherapy.* Wellingborough, Northamptonshire, England: Thorsons Publishers, Inc., 1983.

Tisserand, Robert B. *The Art of Aromatherapy.* New York: Destiny Books, 1977.

Valnet, Jean, M.D. *The Practice of Aromatherapy: Holistic Health & The Essential Oils of Flowers & Herbs.* New York, NY: Destiny Books, 1980.

Worwood, Valerie. *The Complete Book of Essential Oils and Aromatherapy.* San Rafael, CA: New World Library, 1991.

Chapter VIII Unification Rituals for Full Moons, Equinoxes, and Solistices

Starck, Marcia. *Women's Medicine Ways: Cross Cultural Rites of Passage.* Freedom, CA: The Crossing Press, 1993.

Starhawk. *The Spiral Dance: Rebirth of the Ancient Religion of the Goddess.* San Francisco, CA: Harper & Row Publishers, Inc., 1979.

Stein, Diane. *The Women's Spirituality Book.* St. Paul, MN: Llewellyn Publications, 1987.

Index